FLOAT ING WOR LDS

GEOFF PARR

The right of Geoff Parr to be identified as the
Author of the Work has been asserted by her in accordance
with the Copyright, Designs and Patents Act 1988.

Floating Worlds © Geoff Parr 2020
Cover design by Harry Richmond and Geoff Parr

Jelly Bean editor:
Shaun Russell
Editorial:
Paul (Pablo) Henry – The Point Edit
Skin Phillips – The Uplands Edit
Eddie Spearing – The Wanaka Edit

*The photo on the back of this book features Ian Cocking, Dave
Furneau, Mark Diprose and Mark Tucker, Les Arcs, 1987.*

Printed and bound in the UK by
Severn, Bristol Road, Gloucester, GL2 5EU

ISBN: 978-1-913637-15-6

Published by
Jelly Bean Books
Mackintosh House
136 Newport Road, Cardiff, CF24 1DJ, Wales, UK
www.candyjarbooks.co.uk

A Dogbyte Books Publication

A rainbow world
Left behind.
A restless sea
Tears of mine.

So the wild cliffs
Say goodbye.
Golden sands
Sit and cry.

A single moment
To say so long.
Poised in time
Forever gone.

Unknown worlds
Or nothing sane.
Floating worlds
From whence he came.

To my dad.

Dedicated to all the fun snowboarders, skaters and surfers on the planet – without whom there would be no apex competitors!

A large thank you to all the family and friends that assisted me in this epic adventure. and in putting this book together. Special mentions go to Pablo, Dave Furneau, Jeremy Sladen, Eddie Spearing, Rob Needham and more for lending me their ears. Also Lesley and Jackson for letting me sit in front of Mo's old computer for hours on end, Jackson's interruptions only reminding me that it is his generations turn now! Diolch.

— FOREWORD —

Eddie Spearing
Co-Publisher of *Snowboard UK*
Magazine 1991 to 2000
Chairman of the British Snowboarding
Association 1988 to 2004

Those days back when...

That age of youth when we and ours created the punk scene, an intrinsic part of those early days of skateboarding; which was all spat from the earlier surfing ethos, all of which were the ammo from which snowboarding fired it's shots. These lifestyle movements were something we were in control of because we (I use the term 'we' as in all those, worldwide, drawn to these bohemian, alternative singular lifestyles) made them out of what we saw, and felt and were inspired to investigate further.

In those early days, Geoff was just that little bit older, only by a few years it must be said, but those years made the difference to his own understanding of the intertwining surf skate snow music he grew up in and was just that little, even deeper, immersed within.

What we explore in this book are the personal

musings of a major part of Geoff's life, living in a world view of sideways standing water derived interests. It was the essence of his thoughts and which moulded his path. Through his abilities as a photographer and a very engaging eloquent writer due to his off-centric perception, he was so very well received at the magazine and then again as he became a calming voice in the national snowboard association, the BSA.

You will enjoy this book at many levels. Although it tells a personal story, and provides a timeline and insight to the birth of snowboarding in the British Isles, so to it weaves an alchemy of the drivers that push us all into a lifestyle we can dabble in, or be absorbed full body and soul.

The limited images available in the book are backed up and expanded upon with the website to go with the book at www.floatingworlds.info

— CONTENTS —

— INTRODUCTION —

'Love is a river. Drink from it.' – Rumi

Water and its many alter egos make planet Earth exceptional to the surrounding universe, along with our opportune distance from the sun and our unique atmosphere.

Water is soft and fluid yet has the power to wipe out villages, cities, and large populations. It's the source of life and the gangster of violent death, written in simplistic school text as 'H2O', a few mad molecules, kinky by nature. Then, even more mysteriously, it can be as hard as ice, as soft as fluffy snow, as majestic as billowing clouds, as bi-polar as hot steam or as ethereal as a misty morning. It is claimed to be the source of life despite its impulsive path around the planet. A playful provider and a wicked undertaker.

If you live in, on, or by water, in any form, you should know that you have to treat it with respect. The ancient Andaman islander's culture deemed that they should not live close to the water's edge. This advice was transmitted from generation to generation. Centuries later they suffered little loss of life in the devastating Indian Ocean tsunami, thanks to this cultural pearl. Modern civilisation ignores these subtle boundaries and wisdom that operates on a different perspective and timescale. Water molecules collect together to form the vast oceans that dominate our planet. Yet the oceans float on Earth, the earth's crust floats on molten rock, and the planet floats in space. Truly a series of floating worlds, precariously and strangely balanced.

And, at a human level, our bodies are mostly made of water and our lives can drift just like jellyfish in the ocean, as we floppily allow external forces to steer us. However, as we spend nine months floating in the womb this should not be a surprise. Maybe the shock of being dragged out of our watery birth world demands a yearning for something similar. Are we secretly hoping to drift to our inevitable dream destination, or is drifting it?

And why does it feel sensational to surf across the ocean or to snowboard over pristine floaty powder? Could it be that they are exactly the same places? Just glimpses of floating worlds that we came from or belong to. Floating worlds connected to us but long forgotten about just like our births; perhaps the body remembers, if the mind forgets. Floating worlds hidden from us around corners in time and space, our bona fide unknown destination.

What was a surprise though, in my mundane world, was that a simple act by a dog playing in the sea radically changed my drifting life! Almost like some God given master plan. Was the dog in on it? Or does the wind blow flotsam and jetsam across the oceans, to who knows where, totally randomly? Maybe my friend, Mike 'Peanut' Turner, was right about the 'Pinball of Life,' and it was my time to flip the ball and let my life bounce around like crazy! If the answer is blowing in the wind, then it was not visible, and anyway why would I be in a dog's stray master plan?

2

— THE BRAZEN BITE —

'I refuse to be bored.' – Pakey

It was a very hot summer and even my pen was sweating. I was staring at an appalling plan scribed onto a parchment conveyance, badly 'drawn' by some boy clerk in another lifetime. The sloppy red edging around someone's property looked like lipstick, and with the overpowering heat my mind drifted off into a daydream. Unusually for Swansea it was seriously overheating in the office and the seventies decade was providing some great weather. A phone call jerked me back to reality. It was Chris Pake, or Pakey as he was usually called, ringing to say that he was fed up with fixing Land Rovers in the dust so was going to the beach. I could picture him, a whirl of arms, swearing, sweating, tools flying through the air as he attacked a busted vehicle. I was there in an instant, anything but work, so I managed to get myself away early.

We gathered a few more wilting people on the way and drove to Caswell Bay on the Gower and piled into the cooling shiny sea – bliss!

Caswell Bay is very beautiful and looks quite different at high tide compared to low tide. Today it looked like high tide framed with reptilian limestone emerging from the surreal blue sea. The rock layers quickly merge into greenery that rises high above the bay. As the tide ebbs it

3

reveals smooth, clean, yellow sand and some Gaudi-type rock formations hidden around the corner.

An Oxford professor, in a Panama hat, I chatted to over a latte years later told me it was like a cathedral, while he painted the bay for the umpteenth time. The bay is divided into two main parts, w-shaped, and as the sea withdraws people stroll down the sand and stand at the water's edge. They stare out to sea like they are praying, or horizon gazing for their loved one. He described the chancery and other medieval church parts to me, and had clearly put a lot of thought into this bay.

What surprised me today, though, was that the sea was calm and mirror-like but there were regular, spaced out walls of water coming in. These aquamarine smooth waves broke into bright bubbling white water that ran across the face of the wave until all the blue and green had been eaten up. This added another dimension to just swimming. I ran for the lilo and went dizzy blowing it up in my haste to get in. Once we had caught a few waves on it we were having some serious fun, or so we thought. Everyone was enjoying the lilo more than the swimming.

Pakey had brought the dog with him. How do you describe a dog with more character than most humans? It was a long-haired black Border Collie, a large male, inspiringly called 'Blackie'. The dog was a part of our larger tribe and had lived in a lot of homes. Being with Pakey was proving to be one of Blackies mistakes as neither were home birds and struggled to form the proper human-dog relationship. They both had the same thick black hair and freewheeling outlook on life. When Blackie decided to temporarily live at our home I would take him to the local park. Sometimes he would happily tow my daughter in her little car, up and down the playing fields, but that was not enough exercise for him. If I opened the front door he would shoot out and run three miles to town to see the boys living in Carlton Terrace, in a big-shared house. Or he would go chasing a bitch in heat. Navigating the streets was easy for Blackie and I suspected that he regularly called in at the fried chicken shop on the scam. However, Blackie knew that the Carlton Terrace boys always fed and entertained him until someone picked him up.

So Blackie was as excited to be in the sea as we were. To prove it he barked at us catching the waves, often running just before a wave broke on his head. It was great fun until Blackie's excitement got the better of him, and he took a bite at the lilo and the air rapidly fizzed out! The atmosphere changed once our inflatable fun had gone. Someone swore at Blackie, and we mooched about in the water.

Shortly afterwards I saw a work colleague coming down the beach. His nickname was 'Peanut,' and he was always tanned and outdoors. He had sun-bleached hair and a happy round face. He had a large white surfboard under his arm, and as we chatted I explained our predicament, and he kindly said we could try his board after he had surfed. *Game on, this would be a new experience*, I thought.

We watched him go further out than we had been and sit like a Polynesian native looking at the horizon. Then, when a bigger wave appeared, he would turn and paddle furiously.

Jumping to his feet everything changed. He became a

graceful dancer gliding across the face of the wave and always just in front of the breaking white water. It was magic to watch, but the apprehension built as time went on. Maybe it would be more difficult to master than it appeared. In the expert's hands it looked fairly easy.

He clearly enjoyed his session and had probably cut it short for us, as the changing light was hinting at a lovely sunset to come. He briefly explained to us the basics of lying prone on the board and how to paddle. We were strictly told not to attempt to stand up yet!

I paddled out quickly getting flushes of water energy on the way. Full of mixed emotions I turned for a good-sized wave.

What happened then was greater than words can explain. I had taken a step into a different world. My mind was freed without the use of alcohol or drugs.

It was strange that since I had left school I had drifted into most things. I had tried the London commuter life and saw no future in it for me. And then a year spent travelling on the well-trodden path around Europe and Morocco, as a spiritual layabout. That was a fun, but held no sustainable future that I could visualize. Finally I had settled to family life with a stable but boring job, but now I had briefly experienced the surfing thing, and it was powerful.

Like an addict's first hit I was high on a dynamic force that was the power of the wave; the surreal shapes and colours the sea produces and using my body to do something physical. Thanks to Blackie and Peanut I was in a new place.

After catching loads of waves and being in a stunning sunset, which tinted the grey limestone into a tangerine dream, we reluctantly returned Peanut's board to him, with thanks. His board sped along with the precision of a sports car. Pretty different to the ripped piece of material pretending to be a lilo and about to go in the bin! We sat and watched fish rising and the shiny reflections in the waves and translucent green light coming through them, and then the orange ball slid into the sea. *Why couldn't it be like this all the time,* I pondered, and what distant God had sent these walls of water today?

The hypnotic spell was broken by thirst and hunger. As on many hot summer evenings we retired to the pub. We all felt reinvigorated by the sea and sun, but Pakey and I we knew we had found something much more important in our lives. Our occasional glances confirmed that to each other, we were in a state of bliss. Neither of us were eloquent with words so didn't bother to try and inadequately explain what had just happened. We just sat in the glow of a deep happiness that had unexpectedly encompassed us from another world. From Peanuts' perspective, we had just been unexpectedly flipped around by his theoretical pinball of life. A new connection had just been made to another world, and I was flippantly unaware that I was about to go on a long pinball ride. Even in my doubly happy state.

CHAPTER TWO — 1977 to 1984

— THE APPRENTICESHIP —

'Bring on the nubiles.' – blurted by
Pakey during lulls in the pub

In the early days of our surfing we formed a loose band of brothers, consisting of friends from our social network that also caught the surfing bug. Pakey, Jonesey (both called Chris or the 2-Chris's), and Chow. We had other souls that came and went. Our weekends were planned around the BBC weather chart. Would there be any waves, what would the wind be doing and where would the tide be? In the long days of summer it was possible to go in the evenings after work. And this left you feeling happy, tanned and fit. Work became less of a chore as daydreaming about waves kept the boredom at bay.

We surfed whenever we could, even in bad conditions. The beaches we frequented were on the beautiful Gower Peninsula and the vast west facing Llangennith was the usual place to go. However, we would go to the industrial beach at Aberavon and surf in the shadow of the chimneys and smoke of the steelworks. Then we would also make the trip to the barren wilds of Pembrokeshire and surf empty pristine beaches. We saw amazing coves and beaches and just as many rural pubs! Our alternative knowledge of the beaches of South Wales, and how waves broke on them, expanded rapidly. Luckily, Pakey's work took him to British Steel sites and other private places. Sometimes he would quietly say, over a beer, that he had seen an amazing shaped wave on a no-go beach. We would then work out how to get access to these places. We slowly became connoisseurs of the Atlantic's oscillations and strange beaches.

As the seasons changed it became hard work paddling out in winter waves in the cold storms. To keep warm we had to buy cheap diving wetsuits made by Spartan, and the inappropriate suits made us feel spartan. We finally splashed out on proper surfing wetsuits for flexibility and credibility, after a winter of discomfort. However, due to cost we had secondhand boards, and I was so proud of my first one. A yellowy-orange, six foot missile with a little swallowtail and stingers, whatever they were! A logo on the nose declared that it was an 'Island Style,' which evoked the mystical Pacific islands that drove surfing. It had more prestige in my eyes than my car! I considered it a mode of transport just like Pakey's blue minivan that we would pile into, cramped and uncomfortable while he drove at breakneck speed to the beach. On some of the winter days we would get changed on the beach in howling gales or even in the snow! But every good session was rewarded with the surfer's high, well almost!

Since that first ecstatic session caused by Blackie I often tried to analyse what these powerful feelings created by surfing were? I realised that waves were not just pulses of storm energy, each had its own journey story to tell, which influenced how you could ride along it. Additionally these energy swells acted like lenses that focused and intensified those oceanic emotions to unexpected levels. An external voyage along the face of a blue wave that awakened something internally that in turn exploded inside you like a saline bomb, leaving you in a much better place than normal life would.

Even amongst surfers it was rare to try and define what exactly this feeling or experience was. Usually the discussion was about the difficulties faced at surf breaks that had been encountered, or the amazing rides that certain breaks could provide for you around the world. The essence of the addiction went unspoken and when someone tried in, for example, a magazine interview it just sounded lame, much like so many second-rate love songs did.

We slowly learned the art of getting through the waves to the safe area outside where you could get your breath back. Taking off on the waves was a mental battle between fear and fun. The bigger the waves the more the fear froze your senses. Surfing over rocks added to this fear. It is a tough apprenticeship learning to surf but the rewards are great, one big surreal ride, along a wave bigger than yourself as it unwinds, is enough buzz to last for days.

Learning how to surf was a part of the fun. There were no surf schools like nowadays; it was trial and error as you could fall off your board in any direction.

And as each day provided different sea conditions, the consistency of waves varied extremely. This meant that it took years to be able to ride across the wave gracefully with smooth turns – a feat that eluded many.

As the years passed we had gradually become a part of the local surf culture, but were never at the centre of it. We seemed to be on the peripheral edge of an indefinable social wave and were still townies in the eyes of the 'in' crowd. Probably because our other spare social hours were spent with the town crowd, frequenting some of Dylan Thomas's pubs and The Tenby.

Pakey knew every part to a Land Rover and repaired them on muddy sites for a living when he wasn't partying, chasing women and surfing. For him surfing was there to ensure that there was no chance of boredom. Partying and women were his first priority as he swore that on the night that he was born the moon turned a fire red. He was a self-cofessed voodoo child who lived fast and intended to fully enjoy his time on Earth, at whatever cost. He was much like the restless sea that he had now taken to his heart. On the other hand I leaned towards the 'live fairly fast, die oldish and make a reasonable looking corpse.' Our differing backgrounds and outlooks somehow drew us together in an easy relationship that I never fully understood.

On rare occasions, while navigating narrow country lanes, Pakey would snigger to himself and I wouldn't know what was coming next. Sometimes it would be an amusing story like the mouse that got wedged in the coffee machine at work and spent months filtering the coffee. Other times he would confide in me a snippet of his previous night's sexual adventure. I would either grimace or laugh in response. He would have given Casanova a run for his money. He also had a habit of suddenly singing a song line out loud, as if he was singing the rest of the song in his mind. 'What's that in the shadows?' or 'They ain't gonna stick another needle in me,' would suddenly fill the vehicle. Then silence.

He later bought an ex-Land Rover ambulance, which had loads of room for changing into our surf apparel and storing surfboards. However, he continued to drive it like a sports car down the Gower country lanes, and managed to make it through gaps that looked impossible. I bought an orange VW van from Amsterdam and Peanut converted it for me, and Jonesey bought a big Daimler that pulled eyes at the beach. Holidays were mostly taken in Cornwall, discovering the beautiful coves, pasties and pubs. We were living the grey-blue dream.

After many years surfing though, I still didn't consider myself a real surfer. The day that I felt that I had become a surfer happened at a beautiful beach in Cornwall called Constantine. A work colleague from Plymouth, Mike, had turned me on to this beach. I had gone back one autumn with my wife and daughter. The waves were huge and Constantine itself was not surfable as the swell had lost its shape on the shallow reefs and sandbanks. Across the north side of the bay was a long rocky headland that defined one side of Booby's Bay, named I think after breasts! The waves were pushing off the headland and forming a massive peak. The wave then peeled a long, long way parallel to the rocks and finally exploded onto the beach. I wanted desperately to get out through the wild surf but fear was holding me back. I had to work out how I could get out, surf and survive. There were no locals out there for support as they had probably found a more sheltered wave. I was ready after half an hour of visualising and hesitating, then luckily, a surfer from the Townhill area of Swansea rolled up, and he decided to try it too. This new arrival gave me more confidence and buoyed me up.

We both paddled out into the turmoil. The ocean swells felt like a herd of elephants passing slowly underneath us, as we rose up the faces of the waves, over the tops and down the backs. The sounds of the wind and sea were like wild ocean jazz. The land regularly disappeared between the sets of large waves. There was a stiff breeze and occasional sunburst shards through the clouds. There were no other people visible anywhere, and we ended up a long way from our starting point on the beach. I knew this was what I considered as real surfing, and as a result fear and adrenaline were vying for attention.

It was all about positioning myself for a clean take off on the moving saline lump. We paddled around and around and sometimes frantically out to sea, to avoid being pummelled by a giant wave. Then you had to paddle back in to get ready for the 'right wave.' The right wave was about allowing you to ride it safely, and there weren't many right waves that day.

Reading waves is a really important part of surfing, and watching the changing shades of green or grey in their faces informed you what the wave was going to do next. They don't all neatly peel off like an unfolding song. So we spent half an hour paddling to get lined up and I finally saw MY WAVE.

It rose up and blocked out the horizon with a shape like a saltwater mountain. I was on the rocky side of the huge wedge of a wave but felt I could make it across. I paddled hard for what seemed like ages, and then it suddenly picked me up with a ferocious force. I angled the board across the wave whilst jumping to my feet and passed respectfully, in awe, under the peak, almost in surreal slow motion, to the safer side of the wave. Before I knew it I was dropping down the face like a stone. I could see dimples on the face of the wave and funny foam shapes, and below me the greys and blues mingled together in abstract mosaic ways. I carved a bottom turn and rode back up the monster feeling the waves awesome power through my feet. There were tons of water pushing me along at breakneck speed. I was flying!

This continued for hundreds of feet while time froze momentarily, until the wave got close to the beach and became steeper. By then I could no longer ride up and down the face but had to stay at the foot of the wave. And like a great song there was a crescendo coming, and every molecule of me was tuned into the wave and what it was doing. At the same time my spirit was flying free. I looked up at the huge steep wall in front of me and waited for it to annihilate me. But this was my wave, and I flew across the face just as it collapsed behind me, like a chasing freight train. I briefly had time to admire this beauty of nature rising high above, as it was getting ready to thrash the land and myself. It finally shot me into the shallows with a thunderous explosion, and I spun around in the white water rinse cycle, that all surfers know so well. Finally I crawled up the beach breathless. I hugged the sand with my abandoned board dragging on its umbilical cord-like leash behind me. I held onto our planet as it spun steadfastly on its secret orbital mission, travelling through space and time. I was at one with it for a brief moment, and I could even feel it spinning.

Our floating world somehow connected to my surfing, floating world. It was then that self-awareness got its firm grip on me, I coyly checked to see if anyone was watching, luckily they weren't. A deserted beach. I looked back at the hundreds of metres that I had covered in a corner in time. I could see my friend, the bobbing dot, still out there waiting for *his* wave. What a phenomenal ride, this was what I had been working towards for all those years. I would replay the ride over and over in my mind for months and marvel at how that wave could be so heavy and so sublime at the same time. I retired for a huge pastie and pot of tea reward before I could venture back out and maybe blight a great memory of an amazing ride.

Over the years my close surfing friends seemed to wane a bit, but I remained as dedicated and even my salty blood had become tidal. Then Jonesey started to frequent Oz, backwards and forwards like a butterfly, and he planned to move there permanently and stopped surfing. Pakey continued his wild lifestyle, which frequently conflicted with surfing. Many years later, he would succumb to lung cancer and, ironically, he had a choking fit in the bath and drowned in it! And that's after facing all that the Atlantic could throw at him!

Gradually I went on my own more often or sometimes with a young trendy friend from Swansea town called Mark Bowden. Mark's looks and clothes sense resulted in me being almost fashionable, and he pushed me for fitness. We surfed on Mondays as I had gone part-time, and he was off work from selling clothes. For some reason we had many 'Big Mondays,' rather than *'Big Wednesdays'* as made famous by the film. The weekend crowds had disappeared back to work, and we had the sea to ourselves. And the wave God deemed that the weekenders wouldn't share our large, glassy waves. We had some amazing sessions with memorable smooth, green waves and plenty of laughs at our disastrous wipe-outs. We even surfed Christmas mornings for many years, and then went for a traditional pint before lunch. We bounced off each other's personalities.

We were on nodding terms with the surfing population and were friendly with most of them. There was a buzzing vibrant surf scene in Swansea's multi-layered onion world at that time. It was centred around the Langland Bay Hotel, and one individual who had made the world circuit and was the toast and envy of the Swansea scene.

Carwyn Williams was a youngster that had put his body on the line to perform aerials and fantastic manoeuvres on steep waves. He had worked his way into the competition world to the highest level, and gained a lot of respect by the best surfers in the world. Quite amazing considering the location that he had learned in compared to the Hawaiians and Australian professionals. Although as comparable to us town surfers was a full on character from inner Swansea called Felix Halpin. He had excelled at surfing at an early age and won the European Junior Championships in 1972. He was a familiar site in town getting on a bus with his surfboard, which often involved an argument with the bus conductor. Felix had style and grace on a board and travelled the world partying and surfing, with the emphasis on partying!

Our favourite homely evenings involved me cooking a complex Indian curry and Mark bringing the Double Dragon ale around. We would relax afterwards with a surf movie, one of the films that we often watched was an old one, made in 1976 called *Playgrounds in Paradise,* and a part of it captivated me. The middle section of most surf films at that time usually had a wacky snow sequence, and this one duly cut from warm Hawaii to a cold snowy mountain.

Then a subtitle proclaimed 'The Winterstick,' while a person appeared riding effortlessly down a beautiful snow covered wooded mountain. The ride was graceful and went on for ages as he wound through pine trees and deep snow undulations. Sprays of white powder cascaded out at every turn in slow motion, like powerful first stirrings.

This image stuck in my mind, not aggressively but steadily drawing me like a magnet towards it. A seed had been sown in my subconscious mind. Every time that I watched the sequence it meant more and more and more to me, every time. However, it took a few years to do anything constructive about my new daydream... as is my way. Or could it be that Blackie the dog was laughing at me, as I was probably still in his master plan?

CHAPTER THREE — 1985

— LEARN TO LOVE AGAIN —

'I hate anything different.' – short board surfer

By now it was another decade, the bubbling eighties. Summers were fun, but winters were still tough for surfing. Then along came several falls of snow allowing me the opportunity I had been patiently waiting for.

I looked at the shape of the snowboards being used in America by watching videos and studying the occasional magazine. Pictures of snowboards were very rare at the time so I bought a good British surf magazine called *Surf Scene*. In 1985 it included an article on snow-surfing, in which the writer rode in France with the board maker of a brand called Surf Neige. The pictures of the powder riding were excellent, but I couldn't clearly see the shapes of the boards that they were riding. So from all the shapes gathered in my mind I drew up a hybrid sketch and rushed around to see a friend called Roy. Roy had married a lovely work colleague of mine called Sharon, and he was an expert kitchen fitter and a designer... perfect! Some days later we came up with a prototype. Pointed nose, little swallow tail and made of layers of plywood, with a kitchen worktop laminated on the bottom for speed! He managed to steam a bend in the nose and glue it firmly, to retain its shape. We put some windsurfing straps on it to secure each foot, and I was very happy.

The snow was drawing me closer.

A lovely couple I knew often went skiing, and although I had absolutely no desire to ski, I listened excitedly to their tales. Working with Sian I got to hear about huge moguls and heliskiing in Canada. Her husband Rhydd was into anything that involved speed, and he told me that there was a good spot in the Brecon Beacons, and they were going there this weekend. I jumped at the chance, as I was more than ready.

My kit consisted of pinky-red surfing tracksuit trousers with *Edge* Magazine printed on them; a surf hoody and moon boots, not forgetting my unstylish woolly hat. Conversely they had their serious ski gear, so I was undoubtedly on another steep learning curve.

We met at their chosen spot, with a couple of friends. It was cold but invigorating, and there was something fresh and exciting about it. You could feel every breath and see it unfurl through the air. The ancient scenery was disturbingly beautiful as the distant white mountains were quilted with dark patchworks of pine forests. Sensual shapes and shadows were hiding isolated farmhouses, and a moody, dark ribbon of black reservoir water-eyed us coldly. This seemed to be a world far away from the beach.

We chatted and they got kitted up; but I had

nothing to do in my totally sub-standard gear. The plan was to walk up to the mass of vegetation poking out of the snow much higher up and then come down fast. I liked it, simple.

The walk quickly took your breath away. I carried my board under one arm as I stumbled up the hard, slippery snow. It hadn't yet occurred to me that this was not the same snow I had seen in the video. I was so naïve!

They managed to put their skis on with a lot of grunting and clicking, and then slid away gracefully, making little turns before pulling to a stop at the barbed wire fence. Magic. Now they got ready to watch me. The butterflies had suddenly arrived in my stomach from nowhere, and I started thinking that I had no idea of what was about to happen next. This was a giant step into the unknown, so I guessed I had to just ride the snow like it was a wave. Yes, of course, so blatantly obvious! I pointed the board down the hill and it took off like an E-type Jag, catching me unaware. I flew down the slope incapable of turning or even thinking! Everything in my vision was a blur. I was at the bottom in the blink of an eye, so I chose a pile of snow to crash into just before being egg sliced by the barbed wire fence. The board flew off and rode itself, quite happily without me, under the fence into the car park.

I grinned at Sian and Rhydd from the snowy ground. 'I think that the base is too fast' I quipped and glanced at Roy the designer, who had already realised this when he went through the air looking like a flamenco dancer on his first run! Well at least they were having a laugh at my expense, and we immediately bee-lined back up the snowy, icy slope.

Roy and I had fixed little right angles of metal to the edges theorising that they would grip the snow. I had also seen these developments in some of my magazines, however I felt like the board rode more like a freight train on a track – one directional. This meant that turning was not an option, so I later found out to my misfortune.

We spent an hour going up and down the slope, and I got used to the speed and could stop at the bottom ungracefully. Suddenly, the wind began to howl, and the weather was closing in while the temperature plummeted, so we decided a last run was in order. I took off at an angle across the fall line to try and master at least one good turn. It was a bad move and I ended up too far across the slope, where a large clump of frozen vegetation greeted me and immediately grabbed the edge of my board. I was catapulted high up in the air above the frozen ground, lost my balance, and I came down sideways and shoulder charged the planet. Wham! The stuffing was knocked out of me, and my body shuddered. The pain spread through my arm and shoulder as I attempted to get up. I pretended it wasn't much but I still felt pain on and off for six months afterwards.

We sat in the cars and had hot tea and biscuits, while discussing the performance of the board. There was no doubt that it was back to the drawing board or give up! Rhydd explained that the snow was icy and hard and not really suitable for beginners, especially considering the steep terrain! Through my pain though, exhilaration shone like a diamond, and I knew that I wanted to go downhill forever. Just like we had taught ourselves to surf I now had no choice but to learn in the school of hard knocks. And the knocks were harder in snowboarding, but the harder they come...

— IMAGES —

'Don't mention the shark!'–
Lawrie Grove, windsurf instructor

During the early surfing years I had resurrected my dusty photography skills. I wanted to frustratingly try and capture what it felt like to surf. I enjoyed the taking of the photo, but the results never matched the feeling that I was trying to portray. To attempt to improve my photos I bought a serious underwater camera to get a better result. I went to several world contests in Newquay, Cornwall, but actually, I realised that I preferred to surf myself when it was good rather than take shots.

So somehow I got into taking windsurfing pictures, which was more photogenic, due to the colourful sails. Prior to his final move to Oz, Jonesey and I learned to windsurf on flat summer days and dabbled in the blossoming sport. Locally, a hardcore group were going out in big swells and high winds. Horton Beach, on the Gower Peninsula, was a great set up. Powerful side winds with good waves ignited a high-energy session of wave riding and big air jumping as they screamed across the bay. A double thrill. Paddling out on a surfboard is a chore to be endured, but whizzing out on a windsurfer is pure adrenaline.

I would sometimes shoot from the beach or swim out with an inflated Land Rover inner tube for protection, courtesy of Pakey. The windsurfers would buzz me, jump over me or give me a close shave. It was very exciting. Even when a seal would pop up and eye me as a rival or mate!

Lawrie Grove taught us the basics of windsurfing and was at the epicentre of a vibrant scene. I would shoot fun sessions, competitions and visiting top professionals from other parts of the UK. They were mainly drawn by curiosity to see what the hell was going on, but also to have a very good time. Out of the local crowd one young lad stood out from the rest. Keith Sulsh was in his mid-teens and was already taking off on waves and somersaulting himself and the windsurfer in a loop. There were only a handful of people in Europe doing this at that time. He was crazy in and out of the water and had an attitude; push the boundaries and try anything once. We worked together well in the water as I wasn't afraid of getting hit by his board, and he wasn't afraid to hit me. I took a few knocks but generally managed a well-timed duck underwater.

Keith had always struggled with the restrictive confines of competition but excelled in free sessions. One day we went to the vast Llangennith beach in a force nine gale in bleak, grey, damp weather. I swam out with the camera as he fought with his wildly flapping sail. When he finally managed to get control of his rig, he screamed across the sea at breakneck speed and hit a large wave. He went so high I feared he would never come back! He let go of the windsurfer at the zenith of his leap, and it blew one hundred metres along the bay. With his legs and arms flailing, he fell like a stone and landed next to me. It was hilarious. I couldn't stop laughing whereas, on the other hand, he couldn't stop swearing. We survived a bit longer but stopped before there were any serious injuries, and before the wind had sucked all of the energy out of us. My brother Chris was on holiday and had come along to the stormy beach to watch the epic proceedings. When I swam in he declared, shouting into a gale on the deserted beach, us both crazy and maybe he was right as I glanced into Keith's mad eyes!

But what was more important to me, than these insane outings, was that Keith was showing an increasing interest in my snow exploits. Fortunately, he had an involvement with a renegade surfboard factory known as 'Wave Graffiti'. The very name Wave Graffiti summoned an image of a punk surfer slashing graffiti across the face of a blue wave! They had caused a stir in Swansea by breaking away from the earlier established surfboard factory of 'Crab Island'. Wave Graffiti had made Keith's super light windsurfing boards and had developed the shapes from Keith's own feedback. I needed to make better snowboards, and Keith needed another direction to his adrenaline quiver.

So we finally got together and began work on new shapes for the snowboards. My first board had been too short and fat, too stiff and just too crap all round to perform on icy snow. We began to design a better shape and then proceeded to build it with layers of plywood and fibreglass. We tried putting three Velcro straps on it to hold down each foot. These would also allow your foot to rip free in extreme pressure, although that was not always a good thing. We added a bit of fancy paintwork; I had an emergency stop button painted on mine. And we were ready. As a total beginner my enthusiasm allowed me to see these options, but a lot of other ideas would turn out to be dead ends, most of which anyone with any experience already knew. But blimey, did we go down some dead ends!

This new shaped board definitely performed better than the first effort, but I was not yet happy with it. We managed a few sessions in varying conditions and knew deep down that we needed another design. However, we did not really know what we needed yet, as we had discovered many different shaped boards being used in America. Maybe this was the future direction?

CHAPTER FIVE — 1985

— GOOFY OR REGULAR? —

'I could not help concluding that this man felt the most supreme pleasure while he was driven on so fast and so smoothly by the sea.' – Captain James Cook

A few weeks prior to a good snowfall I was sat on my surfboard way out at sea, feeling the strong oceanic pulse. It was a big day at Llangennith beach, and mercifully no wind to spoil the waves, but the waves were hard to catch. This was due to the faces of the waves being not quite steep enough on the approach, so you had to be in the exact right place to catch one just seconds before it broke. This swell was much like a piece of music that rises up very slowly and then explodes into a sudden crescendo. Sitting safely outside of the breaking waves I drifted off into daydream mode with the sun on my face, magically charging some internal battery. *So where had these board sports originated from?* I pondered to myself.

Firstly, they all involved riding in a sideways stance. When you first try standing sideways on a board you automatically choose whether your left leg or right leg leads. Strangely, approximately seven in ten people stand with their left foot planted forward. So this became known as regular or natural foot stance. The remaining riders preferred to stand with their right foot in the forward position and were known as goofy footers, but paradoxically it doesn't seem to have any bearing on which hand you mainly use in daily life.

Standing sideways, like a Samurai warrior, helps your balance and enables more powerful turning, as you try to race across the wave ahead of the curl. The downside in surfing is that you may have to ride a wave with your back to it as you go across it. Vision and posture make it more difficult to react accordingly to the changing wave and therefore any turn off the wave face is harder. Conversely riding facing the wave is easier and much preferred generally by surfers.

According to historical journals, surfing developed many centuries ago, maybe in various parts of the world in some form or other. However, Hawaii was where the earliest written records were recorded about native islanders riding waves on boards. But it wasn't the Hawaiians that recorded it, as they had no written language when Captain James Cook came across them in 1778. He was, however, bowled over by their surfing skills and recorded some wonderful descriptions in his journal at the time.

Surfing spread slowly around the world, the trend took off dramatically in the early 1960s with California and Hawaii being the epicentre of this new lifestyle. Changes from traditionally carved wooden boards to the modern era materials, such as fibreglass and foam, made surfboards much lighter and easier to manoeuvre. As a result, surfing became more accessible to a much wider public audience around the globe. The equipment evolution exploded.

Next came the spin-offs. The Californian surfers came up with the idea of the skateboard for practising their surfing moves on, when the waves were flat. Windsurfing was later developed by surfers to ride in waves. Early snowboarding began to appear in backcountry America, as surfing-inspired pioneers wanted to surf the snow in the same fashion as waves. And so it evolves. With surfing at the core, these other sports became the medium for imaginative people to get their surf high. This could apply despite the fact that they lived far away from the ocean. The ocean's children were exploding into differing subcultures, and interestingly for me the equipment had to change its size and shape.

Each discipline rooted in surfing took on its own direction and development in terms of equipment and culture, and standing sideways was at the heart of these cosmic cousins, with centrifugally induced highs from power linked turns. Skateboarders began to use dry swimming pools and city streets, which in turn lead to skate parks and as a result the later development of the hardcore street scene and culture. Windsurfers began to attain incredible high speeds, race on courses and even cross challenging oceans. Some of these disciplines overlapped with sailing, but some still stayed with the waves....

'Hey, your wave, mate!'

Suddenly someone shouted at me. I snapped out of my pensive trance just in time to see a huge mountain of water about to break on top of me. I was the only one in a position good enough to catch it, despite some urgent paddling by nearby surfers.

I panicked.

Then I realised that it would not look good enough to my salty peers if I didn't go for it. I turned and paddled, hoping the wave would slip under me. It didn't and I jumped to my feet, and then dropped rapidly down the face with shaking legs. I made it to the bottom and turned hard left, so as a goofy footer, the watery monster would be face on. To my absolute astonishment, a surprisingly smooth and beautiful ride unfurled before me. High and full of false bravado I paddled back out to my spot in the ocean, somehow expecting some appreciative comments from my captive audience. However, no one gave me a second glance; that's surfing! Deep down, I knew that if I hadn't gone for it they would have tutted and stared at me.

Crisis over I sat on my board, far out the back in a sea of lost thoughts and began to dwell on snowboarding a bit more. At the time I knew little about snowboarding and its development in America. I had heard about a 'snurfer', more of a toy board with no foot straps and a rope to hold on to, attached to the nose. I later found out that half a million snurfers were sold from the mid-sixties to the late-seventies. The Winterstick that I had seen in the movie *Playgrounds in Paradise* was from Utah, and made by someone called Dimitrije Milovich and seemed to be the best board in the States. It's shape was like a compressed surfboard. In addition I had seen pictures of a board made by someone called Jake Burton; this design looked like it was an extension of the snurfer. I decided then and there that I wanted something that lay between the two designs. I was taking the middle road, as Buddha said. I caught the next available wave to the beach in an excited frenzy to get designing.

A few weeks later after labouring in the surf factory with Keith, we had our new snowboards but no snow!

Then, like a miracle, the TV weather forecaster pointed to a load of snowflakes over Swansea, and there were snowflakes all over South Wales.

When it arrived, Swansea was unusually covered by more than a few inches of snow. The weather forecast had been correct! Chaos on the roads ensued so driving anywhere was out of the question. I enthusiastically put on my totally inadequate gear and strolled up the road to a nearby park with a short and steep slope. I was accompanied by my daughter, along with my inquisitive neighbour, Kevin, who couldn't resist the fun, as could our snowy coloured dog, Lucy.

The steep park ended with a useful hedge that prevented us from landing in the main road. This snow was softer than that experienced on that first pivotal outing. So I rode down the hill faster and faster, only managing to stop and avert disaster by crashing into the hedge. We took turns at this kamikaze endeavour and Lucy ran alongside barking. Probably trying to tell us that we were barking.

Although it was impossible to make good turns, I found myself able to traverse the slope and change direction. Brilliantly, I could now stop without getting a mouthful of hedge! Also the soft deep snow allowed the board to float silently along, or sometimes with a gentle hissing sound. But nothing had prepared me for what happened next.

A local surfer, windsurfer and photographer had got wind of what I was doing. Paul Gill or 'The Gill' as he was known was chief wheeler-dealer in Swansea's surf scene. Apart from having the biggest moustache, he had arranged for BBC Wales to film surfers entering the water from a snowy beach. This was to be used at the end of the evening news as a fun feature. However, when the camera crew arrived the next snowy morning there were no waves. The Gill, always thinking laterally, immediately put them on to me to film this new craze that hadn't really developed.

So I duly met up with them and the interviewer in the same park, not without some trepidation. They filmed us riding 'kamikaze style,' followed by an in depth interview. At the end of the conversation the interviewer asked me whether it would ever make the Olympics! I was flabbergasted and amused, partly because it was so embryonic and partly because I had a t-shirt from an early surf trip, and compulsory visit to Glastonbury on the way. It had the Olympic rings spread out all over the place and said, 'F*** the Olympics'. In the press at that time there had been many allegations of corruption, bad politics and mismanagement. In that moment, I didn't know what a contentious question that would turn out to be years on! But I couldn't help laughing at his question.

That night I was shocked to see myself being broadcast all over Wales on the BBC evening news! In my hometown of Swansea it brought me instant 'fame' at work and with friends, although most people didn't really understand it. From then on the term 'snowboarding' got confused with 'snowballing,' or 'ski boarding,' by fellow workers and the people that I knew. Years later a young lad, Tudor Thomas or 'Chod' to his mates, from far away North Wales told me that he was just developing an interest, when he saw the item on TV. He was amazed that someone else was dabbling in snowboarding in South Wales. It finally took about a year before I had bumped in to most of my old friends and the TV subject was eventually dropped. However, once I had experienced my fifteen seconds of fame I quickly realised that the power of media exposure did not always have an advantageous effect on your ego, and sometimes the opposite was true.

— FALLING AND FLYING —

'They fall, and falling, they're given wings.' – Rumi

Spring arrived and we were left without any chance of snowy conditions, but by then we had conceived a few more interesting shapes and tried them out on the last of the winter snows. Sadly, there had not been enough time to develop the perfect board, if such a thing existed! However, we continued on our mission relentlessly, and had bought a stiff plastic binding that screwed into the board, which could then be used with moon boots. We approached an engineering company based in the Rhondda Valley to try and produce our own version of the plastic binding, but were shocked by the cost of the mould. It meant that we would have to sell several thousand of them just to break even!

So for our next brainwave, we tried chopping up old ski boots, while retaining a plastic skeleton that supported the back of the leg, and the two remaining straps would fasten your foot into the ski boot. We then bolted the plastic skeleton to the board. This system, when combined with wearing soft moon boots, felt very comfortable and secure. Chomping at the bit, we decided that we had to go and ride somewhere to test the system, and the only place we could think of to simulate snow were large sand dunes. We headed along the coast to a quiet spot that we knew about that had the steepest sand dunes. The only problem with sand is that it obviously creates a lot of friction. This surface friction stops the board from moving fast, so the steeper the dune the better in order to overcome it. However, it was a brutal initiation to this new medium. As the board took off we tumbled, head-planted and even managed to burn the bottoms of the boards. Sand found its way into every orifice and even in our eyes, and it took days to get all of it out!

Being a bit crazy we tried a few more times, before someone told us about an artificial ski slope in Cardiff, great! We rang and got permission to ride there, but were told to only go when it was not busy with skiers.

On arriving at the slope we were greeted with a short, thin, ugly grey giant brush! It looked like a bristling monstrosity, and it certainly wasn't St Moritz! There was a strange lift at the side with long, dangling poles that a few skiers were sitting on to be dragged up. I was flabbergasted, as I expected something much swishier. Oh well, never mind! My friend Keith had skied abroad and knew about these lifts, but I had never encountered one.

He jumped on, and grabbed the pole and took off smoothly up the slope. *That looks easy*, was my first thought, as I stood waiting for a pole to come around to me. I was standing with my board sideways to the slope, and both feet locked on to the board. I grabbed

36

the pole and shot off up the hill, although unbeknown to me, my board had caught the metal base to the brush-impregnated slope. As a result it didn't budge, my body stretched, and my left knee twanged! I was finally forced to let go of the pole, which catapulted away with a springy resonance, and left me lying flat on the floor in agony!

My hurt pride forced me to limp up the slope to the top, where we unhesitatingly strapped the boards on. 'Chocks away then,' I said, and Keith went off fast, veered left and went straight off the ski slope into a nearby hedge! It was my turn to laugh, and I momentarily forgot about my throbbing knee.

Gingerly, I rode straight down the slope, hoping that I wouldn't fall, no turns or fancy stuff whatsoever. Keith tried a few more runs, but went flying up in the air when he also caught the edge of the board on the lethal matting.

After half an hour of torture we hobbled off the slope, and said thanks to the staff, thanks for nothing.

'Shall we find a hospital,' I half joked to Keith who was pulling nylon needles out of his backside. We laughed and relived the experience while driving back, but I knew that my knee was pretty bad.

Over the summer I tried to get my knee back to normal with the help of a specialist. Our windsurfing osteopath, Simon, was forever keeping us mobile, and put a lot of effort into my wounded knee. Undeterred by our painful experience, we continued to design new shapes, resulting in us finally using a fibreglass expert to make a foam core board that would easily pop out of a mould. Without really knowing it, we were getting deeper into the complexities of producing boards.

The next winter arrived upon us quickly and we had made several new boards to try, but I was still limping badly. When the snow arrived on the Brecon Beacons we rushed up, well, I hobbled up the mountains alongside Keith. Keith would then ride down, and I would observe how the board performed, and I would impatiently wait for him to walk back up for a performance review. This was very frustrating for me, but I didn't want to miss any of this journey of development. As it was the foam core board broke into smithereens upon hitting a rock! Yet another dead end, but we weren't about to give up.

By mid-winter I was ready to ride as the muscles around my knee had regained their strength and there was little pain now. Due to the variable weather conditions we would have to hike to wherever we could see patches of snow. Pen y fan, the highest mountain in South Wales, was the most reliable source of snow. In one big blizzard we trudged to the top, in a Siberian-like environment and unsurprisingly saw none of the usual walkers. What we did see though, was the occasional gun print in the snow and the shady SAS training for war, along with a group of modern day Druids having a ceremony on the bleak ridge! The conditions were so atrocious that only the hardy, sorry crazy, were out in it, so I didn't risk riding with my recovering knee in such bad conditions.

For my inaugural run we went to a spot we called *'The Sheep Pens'*, when I was ready to ride again. After hiking up the slope, I savoured the moment while strapping my feet to the board. As I took off the board floated smoothly down the hill with a slight hissing sound, in this otherwise silent landscape. I could feel the solid air around me on this windless blue-sky day, and it was fantastic. Flying like an eagle again and with a board that was much easier to control, I was as happy as the well-fed Red Kite that flew over to inspect us. We had made progress and were extremely happy with the altered dimensions of our latest prototype. We were unable to turn with any style yet but could get around and miss the rocks and plants sticking out of the snow.

In our part of the world the overriding ocean climate would cause the snow to melt quickly or it would get windblown, so we always had to be on top of our game. When the weather cooperated, we would shoot up to Brecon as fast as possible. However, it was exciting and great fun, and we slowly managed to find a lot of 'secret' spots that worked on certain snowfalls. On one occasion we rode long ribbons of snow that had filled in the gulleys due to the high winds. We had even been in the dark with torches, in our quest for the ultimate board. At that time a Swansea-based national magazine existed called *'Edge,'* which printed coverage of surfing, skating and any alternative adrenaline sports. They decided that they wanted to put an article in about snowboarding in the Brecon

Beacons.

As a result I wrote it for them, together with pictures of Keith riding the rare deep snow gullies. They published the article once I had submitted it. Although despite these little bits of media attention, the local surfers were either bewildered or suspicious of what we were doing.

We took family and friends up to the Beacons sometimes, to witness or try this new exciting way to ride the snow slopes. On these glorious blue-sky snowy days we would have a picnic, and my daughter would ride down sat on a board, screaming with delight. On one of these days I dragged Jonesey and his wife, Alison, up with their windsurfing dog, Gwyn. When Jonesey shot down the hill in the deep snow, Gwyn ran after him and in his excitement bit his trailing hand! Blood dripped onto the snow, staining it pink and after this incident Jonesey never came again. In fact he permanently moved to Australia not long afterwards, instead of flitting backwards and forwards like an inebriated butterfly. I asked myself, what is it with dogs? At least Blackie had the decency to just bite the lilo.

A final version of our board was reached, with the help of our fibreglass guru, and the resulting board was constructed with fibreglass all over, along with stronger Kevlar edges. A plywood core and two drilled in butchered ski boots served as bindings. Our chosen brand name for them was 'Snow Shark', and the boards had our logo proudly displayed on them. We even managed to sell half a dozen or so around the country. Rhydd bought one and took it to the Alps on holiday, to try out on the steep slopes of Val d'Isere. Rhydd was always full on, and convinced his wife, Sian, and his mates to try the board. They used instinct, rather than skill, to ride it, but soon found that it was more difficult than it appeared and that skiers would stare at you, with questioning looks! In addition, some top skaters and surfers bought them in other parts of the UK, so we had achieved something, but deep down knew that we had to get our hands on a genuine American-made snowboard one day. That was now the aim, we were amateurs trying to be professionals, and although I continued to go surfing in the milder weather, I always had one eye on the mountains.

CHAPTER SEVEN— 1986 to 1989

— PURE SPIRIT —

*'I have seen the future of snowboarding,
it's not for me.' – Huw Parsons*

A name that kept reoccurring like a whisper in the wind was 'Huw Parsons', and after hearing the name mentioned on a fairly frequent basis, particularly by the skiing fraternity, my curiosity and ego finally caved in. In an attempt to find out who this snowboarder was that instilled such respect amongst his peers, I decided that I would have to go to Cardiff to meet him head on. Any skiers in Swansea, in the know, were aware of a shop in Cardiff called 'Outdoor Action'. It was run by three partners, Dave, Lyndsey and Huw, and was set in the suburbs on a corner, amongst a maze of terraced roads. So it was that I drove up one Saturday morning with the family, drawn to this enigmatic, reputable place. I carried a certain amount of apprehension about this trip as I had no idea what to expect, and it could possibly turn out to be an embarrassing waste of time. All that I knew was that someone there was a snowboarder, and apparently a good one. However, whether or not he wanted to talk to me would be another matter.

After getting lost in the terraced streets we finally

located the premises and walked timidly into the shop, to be greeted by the warm embracing smell of hot wax. There were lots of customers loitering about or indifferently browsing various bric-a-brac dangling from the walls. The three partners were rushing around at breakneck speed, to try and keep up with the demand, and the shop was the proverbial beehive of activity. Despite this, my eyes were quickly drawn to the ski workshop, above which, were two beautiful snowboards on display. They were both early Wintersticks, made by Milovich, and one in particular seemed to jump out at me. This one had a lovely curved profile combined with a long pointed nose and a strange rounded tail configuration. It was also decorated with the image of a lovely woman in sunglasses, backed by a palm tree and a tropical storm. It could have been directly lifted from the petrol tank of a Hell's Angels chopper, and it seemed to add another dimension to the board. The other board was longer and thinner, with narrower hips and ended in a classic swallowtail. I was awestruck, to say the least after what was my first encounter with a real snowboard.

I drank in the boards trying to absorb the curvaceous shapes and imagery, and let my imagination drift as to what they would be like to ride. The curves of the boards were as graceful as a hollow wave and the finish as good as a well engineered Porsche. Mesmerised for at least five minutes, I was suddenly interrupted by a tall dark-haired athlete who approached me, dressed in casual mountain clothing.

'Hi, can I help you?' he asked.

I found myself speechless and totally dumbstruck, I didn't know what to say or where to start. I had found Nirvana and the mysterious Huw Parsons.

Huw flicked his long straight hair aside and listened to my amateur story of snowboarding to date. He calmly asked us all to sit down and he would make us a coffee when it became quieter. In the meantime he flitted backward and forward between the tasks of serving customers, servicing skis, and clipping climbing ropes around optimistic customers. Our conversation was constantly interrupted in order for him to serve customers, but it seemed natural and suited Huw's apparent ethereal character.

I instantly warmed to him, and if he had been my officer in the trenches I would have gladly followed him over the top. He projected an air of serene calmness, and clearly knew a great deal about everything outdoor. Slowly, in dribs and drabs, I learned more about the forefront of snowboarding. In 1983 when the film *Apocalypse Snow* had reached the shop Huw and Lyndsey were spellbound by it, and in addition they became addicted to the background music played by The Art of Noise, in particular a song named 'Moments in love.' Upon seeing the film, without hesitation they had flown to Geneva and headed for the French ski resort of Les Arcs, where they found Didier Lafond, the maker of the film. There and then they bought three Winterstick boards from him, and returned home ready to go on a new adventure. This clever move, to go to the source of their inspiration, set them on a snowboarding path that had not crystallised in the UK yet. After a few further hours of chatting we headed home, with the promise that I could call again and learn more. I was ecstatic and enthused, but the family by now were totally bored!

Over the following months I visited Huw regularly, and I learned that he drove to the French Alps for long weekends with his girlfriend in their Citroen 2CV. He would carefully check the weather, and his destinations were mainly Chamonix and Val D'isere. Once the conditions looked promising, they would make the long, rattling drive overnight and arrive in the French Alps in the morning, shaken but not stirred. He was on a mission to break in new couloirs, steep descents and cliff drops that hadn't been attempted on a snowboard before. His previous mountain climbing experience came in handy to achieve this, as he was able to climb down to snow faces that were otherwise unattainable.

At first I wasn't sure whether he was embellishing these stories that he came back with. Although they intrigued me, I loved them and they fired my imagination to push my own abilities further. Later on he presented me with a load of photos that had been professionally taken of him, alongside a magazine article. There was a picture of him in full flight coming off the roof of a large alpine building, another of a steep couloir being tackled and a vertical cliff jump of at least forty feet. Now that I had witnessed what he was capable of for myself, I was even more amazed. He played down his own persona but he gave off an aura of a life lived on the edge. My only possible criticism of him was to pick holes in his euro-trendy headband, Tonto's expanding headband, no less, but he did have long hair to keep out of his face, I guess I could forgive him this.

He was always trying to help and encourage me, and after many months he offered to sell me his very own board, as he knew that I could not afford to buy a new one. He rode an American made Sims Ultimate, which was a red board with a pointed nose and a swallowtail with rounded U-shape ends. I was already in love with it but had never expected to ride it, and I had already seen what it could do in his photos! We agreed a date for me to pick it up, when his next new board arrived in the shop from America, I couldn't wait.

At this time in the States, however, there was a conflict going on in the emerging board development. Both Huw and Lyndsey had found that the metal skegs on their Wintersticks caught the snow when coming on to the firmer pistes from the soft snow, so they cut them down in order to ride in resorts. This was a similar problem to the one that I had encountered on my first board in hard, icy conditions. Milovich had no ambition to make boards for the hard pistes of ski resorts, and part way through the 1980s stopped producing Wintersticks and moved into designing windsurfers. This left the door open for two new innovators in the sport, Tom Sims and Jake

Burton, who were designing boards for different types of use.

Tom Sims came from a skateboarding background, and had made his name as a skateboard manufacturer, before that sport peaked and went into decline. Around 1978 Sims saw his opportunity in making snowboards for jumping and emulating skateboard moves. With his friend, Chuck Barfoot, development was started on rideable snowboards that were a definite improvement on the snurfer, and more versatile than the Winterstick. This style of snowboarding was generally called 'freestyle', and incorporated many of the existing skateboard manoeuvres.

Around the same time Jake Burton was busy developing snowboards backcountry and particularly for racing, in an attempt to develop the old Snurfer race events. So simultaneously Burton was making boards on the East coast, while Sims was based on the West coast of America. Their natural rivalry was easily fed and resulted years later in a huge court case.

The boards made by Sims were more flexible, which made them easier to ride and the shapes were rooted in skating and surfing. Burton, on the other hand, made stiffer and edgier boards for the crossover skiers and racers. Huw was of the opinion that Sims boards were better in that instant, and I already knew from my trials that it was easy to make a stiff board but difficult to produce one with sufficient springy flex. Sims and Burton, it seemed, were at loggerheads over everything. Burton started competitions with racing events only and Sims forced freestyle to be a part of national competitions. However, this rivalry helped push the sport to new levels, and a cross-pollination of ideas took place.

The day finally arrived for me to collect my dream board, struggling to contain my excitement I hurriedly drove to the shop. Huw spent some time explaining the board to me, and he showed me how to put the bend back into the board, which is known as camber. When the board was laid on its base it should not touch the floor around the central area, but just lay with the nose and tail in contact with the floor. Because of excessive use, the wood has a tendency to give up its natural spring, so he propped it base up between two chairs balanced on the nose and tail. He then, surprisingly, put a pile of books on the centre of the base in order to bend the board. I was told to do this overnight so it was ready for the next day! The base was made of a material called P-tex and regularly needed waxing with hot wax; hence the inviting aroma of their shop. I bought some second hand mountaineer boots in the shop ready to wear on my brand new second hand board. Surprisingly, there were no specific snowboard boots at this time, but some people began using a tall soft Canadian walking boot made by Sorrel, which were softer than mountaineer boots. The board also had proper bindings to strap your feet to the board; I was enthralled and couldn't wait to try them.

It struck me as a mystery that you waxed the bottom of a snowboard for speed, but to stay on a surfboard you rubbed wax onto the top!

The deal done, Huw said that the winter season's new snowboards had just arrived from the States, and I watched feverishly as he opened the packages. Inside there were six Sims boards that were all pre-ordered for the whole of the UK that winter. There were called Sims Blades, and they were coloured red with gold stripes and had sharp pointed noses and a squaretail. I was absolutely amazed, as they looked so futuristic and mean. Besides this delivery, he also had some Burton boards, such as the Burton Safari, which looked very big, and unsurprisingly, with the deck covered in black and white safari stripes. It had a softer shaped nose, long straight edges and a squaretail too, but it was much stiffer. I realised how the graphics on the board were as important as the design of the board. Despite the graphics having no bearing on the performance of the board, they instantly attracted you to it. In addition, they would also help future generations to define each era of snowboarding, soon to be lost, or create a specific memory from a time and place. Like surfboards, snowboards also lend themselves as canvasses to display vivid artwork on, and some eye-catching creations evolved from then onwards.

On reflection, at this early stage, it would have been possible for Huw, Lyndsey and Dave to become the official importers of either brand, with the resulting success this would have brought. Anyway, none of that mattered to me, as I drove home with the board in the back of the car so I could see it in my rear view mirror. Once at home it took pride of place in the living room, just as my surfboard had. When I looked at it I was grateful that Tom Sims had gone through all the problems to produce it, but more importantly I had got my hands on Huw's own board, my new anti-hero.

I managed to meet Huw on several later occasions away from the shop. Once in Val D'isere in the Solaise bar at night, where he drank mineral water and chatted about where he was going on the next days ride. However, at that time it was well out of my league so I didn't get to ride with him. I also met up with him in Merthyr Tydfil, a coal-mining town in the valleys of South Wales. Someone had come up with a great idea to build a lift up the valley side and spray artificial snow on it. Sadly the warming climate soon put paid to it, after they had covered it in snow for one attempt, it rapidly melted away! Plan B was to create a dry slope and so they threw artificial matting on to an ill-prepared slope.

A huge bumpy, twisted slope greeted us with flocks of sheep running across the piste, it certainly felt like the Wild West! Huw flew down the slope riding with so much natural abandon, and on the limits of the artificial brush, while coming close to being caught by the twisted matting. I couldn't believe how precariously he rode, but so gracefully at the same time, whereas, on the other hand, I rode more moderately to save breaking any bones.

As time rolled on Huw never seemed to slow down. He learned to fly a hang-glider so that he could

50

launch off snowy mountains attached to his board. I later heard from the instructor that he was a natural and learnt with ease, and far quicker than anyone that he had ever taught before. As time went on I saw him less and less, as my own world became more hectic. Then I heard a rumour that the shop was going to close or change, so I went to see him sombre at the fact that my favourite shop was possibly going to close. Huw, however, was chatty and excited with his long hair now cut short. He told me that the partnership was about to split up, but that was no problem as he had found sponsorship and was about to train to fly helicopters; no surprise there. He would eventually end up flying workers to the rigs in the North Sea. But one surprising thing that he said to me, that resonated in my sub-conscious, on that day was: 'I have seen the future of snowboarding, it's not for me.'

These words would echo back years later.

Out of all the excellent British snowboarders I saw over the following years, no one was able to display the natural talent that Huw possessed. He just went and took on difficult mountains without a need for an audience to satisfy his ego, and he was not into being tribal. Even more relevant was the fact that he was in the early era, having to use very basic equipment, and having little technical knowledge of riding techniques. He had won the first slalom at the first ever British Snow Championships, even after falling over on the course. In addition, and even more surprising, he had been fifteenth in the first ever World Championships held in Europe after a start number of 210! Starting so late meant that the course was already a churned up mess by the time that he got to ride, and his talents could be smoothly transferred to an array of disciplines. However, for me more important than that, he possessed a spirit that was busting out of him, a pure spirit unhindered by life's drudgery. He was a true individual and explorer in his own right, and without him UK snowboarding would have been the poorer for it. Hardly anything of what he did on a board had been documented; he just seemed to do it in such a quiet and unassuming way. Luckily, I had overcome my reluctance to meet up with him and had spent a few valuable years in his company.

— THE MAGIC SWIRLING STICK —

*'They are banning snowboarding right across
the Alps.' – Swansea ski instructor*

Chatting in the shop with Huw had enabled me
to see a much bigger picture of snowboarding
and its progress. I was also shocked to find out how
far behind Huw I was in riding experience. Progress
in the States had been long and slow while going
from the backcountry soul snowboarders of the early
'70s to the changing scene of the '80s. The original
riders were almost invisible to the ski world, and
they were much more likely to have had hippy green
credentials or mountain knowledge. They avoided
ski runs like the plague, mainly because of the
limitations of the boards, but also because they loved
to ride in fresh powder away from the ski pistes.
Changes occurred when the board makers
incorporated the attributes of ski technology into
snowboards, namely inset metal edges, bindings,
side cut and camber. These comprehensive boards
could then be used all over the prepared ski pistes,
and thus ski resorts became popular playgrounds.
But with one limitation, only where they would let
boarders on!

As the numbers grew and boarders rode a

different line down the slopes, to their fellow skiers, more skier complaints arose. It was different and it attracted a different type of person, often coming from surfing, skating and some wannabe's who quickly latched on to this new pastime. There was also teen spirit and adrenalin bouncing around and this accompanied by their cultures led to foreseeable friction on the slopes. Ski fashion was booming with expensive flouro, tight suits displaying a variety of bright colours, but surfing's laid-back attitude brought its own image along. Urban skateboarding, along with its own fashion and attitudes, also crept on to the scene; the ski clothes didn't feel or look right to most snowboarders.

Because of cultural and attitude reasons, many resorts in America would not allow snowboarders on their slopes. Acceptance for the new way of riding the snow was slow to spread, and at this point the skiing fraternity could have been instrumental in stopping snowboarding ever developing further than a backcountry pastime. Coincidentally skiing's popularity had peaked according to ski demographics, which resulted in declining numbers and income for ski resorts. Money talks. But despite the hesitant acceptance of snowboarders by the resort management, the friction continued for years between some skiers and snowboarders. Whichever side you were on, it was an easy opportunity to wind someone up or reinforce your tribal instincts. Again the earlier alternative view of a lifestyle that had been nurtured by beatniks, hippies and surfers was proved to be alive and kicking. The conflict of two countercultures with mainstream skiers versus the alternative boarders would develop into a very real and pseudo-class struggle, sometimes veiled, sometimes not. The way I saw it was that we were like the flipside of the same coin, but we couldn't see each other!

However, the introduction of snowboarding in Europe occurred later and much quicker than the States. This was partly due to American resorts learning the hard way first and thanks to their growing pains European resort bans were more fiction than reality. Certain ski instructors and skiers saw this new movement as a threat to their perfect lifestyles and tried to undermine it. In France, however, the spirit of 'La Glisse' ensured that you could try anything in pursuit of fun. In those early days of snowboard development I had a postcard from Sian and Rhydd who were holidaying in the French resort of Val d'Isere, and it featured a marvellous cartoon of someone riding down the slope doing a headstand on a snowboard. The caption read 'C'est nouveau!' ('It's new!'). That was the French spirit as regards getting down the mountain, which allowed snowboarding to develop and many of us admired this attitude. Ironically, their closed shop outlook on foreigners teaching on their slopes was in direct opposition to this spirit and lacked any cordial intent.

Funnily enough my first trip to an actual ski resort was a mixed experience. One of the windsurfing crew, an avid skier, had split up from his wife, and he was desperate to go skiing, while I was champing at the bit to try out my 'brand new secondhand' Sims board, purchased from Huw.

So we had flown to the tiny tax-free principality of Andorra, to the resort of Arinsal situated high in the Pyrenees, two people on different missions; one filled with anger and one filled with apprehension and excitement. Although I was apprehensive about the lifts, the steepness of the mountains was an even bigger concern.

We arrived in the dark and clattered into a very large old hotel and hit the sack immediately. The next morning I put my cheap ski gear and mountain boots on and proceeded to carry my board to the bus. The mountains were now visible in the morning light and appeared to be very steep and rocky. I could not see any safe patches of snow to ride on like I was used to back home in Brecon. Even though my stomach had tied itself into a huge knot, I quickly reasoned that it was not their intention for ski tourists to die here and there must be snow somewhere behind the steep cliffs. The bus duly deposited us at a scenic waterfall with a rickety chairlift going straight up and over the falls! This was far more precarious than I thought, and in a final 'coup de gras' my partner suddenly declared that he had lift vertigo.

The lift swung out on takeoff; like a funfair ride. We jumped onto the fast moving wooden slats and took off, while I held onto his back and he focussed on the nearest bit of terrain without looking down. Up and up the waterfalls we went without any snow in sight, just rock and conifers. Finally, the air became colder as we went up over the ridge and we were suddenly welcomed by a huge bowl of gleaming white snow and blue skies. I couldn't believe that I was actually here, it was real, my first ski resort, after all that hiking in the Brecon Beacons. I was aware that my face was tingling with cold and excitement.

Now we had to catch another lift up the bowl now, and the journey seemed endless, as I was so desperate to ride down. We parted company at the top and I admired the view and began to visualise my run down. My thoughts harked back to Huw and what he had done on this board; it must work for me too, I summarised in a hurry!

Strapped in I took off, and the well-waxed board began to fly. The speed allowed me to make nice turns off the small banks, causing me to grin like a Cheshire cat. This was undoubtedly the Rolls Royce of boards in my mind, and I was snowboarding for real. I was oblivious to anyone else on the mountain, and kept repeating the same lift and piste back down, which made my exhilaration soar higher and higher.

However, despite the huge grin on my face, after a few hours I was finally bored of this run, so I decided to try out another route. Following a new sign rewarded me with a beautiful gulley with high smooth sides, like a huge wave on the ocean.

Fantastic, I could now pull surf-style turns off the high-sided walls, and this natural feature curved intriguingly around the corner and then flattened out to reveal a packed restaurant full of eager onlookers. Each run I was able to nonchalantly cruise past the restaurant with a casual grin on my face. This caused loads of lounging, drinking, skiers to stare at me, as in fairness, they had never seen someone flying by on a board before. On one run I even passed a line of beginners being taught by an instructor with his back to me. All the skiers' heads followed me until the instructor himself was forced to turn round. It was truly comical and I loved the brief attention as I whizzed by.

A quick stop for lunch was all I needed, and my new 'admirers' were drinking cheap champagne and beer in rather large quantities. One comical Irish skier from our hotel was firing champagne corks at passing skiers! Not for me though, I still had to carve hundreds of surf turns in the gulley, until the fast descending sun signalled the closing of the mountain. This perfect day only became slightly tarnished when we had to deal with the lift down and my friend's vertigo problem. Back at the hotel I had a big, hot, muscle-relaxing bath and shut my eyes and relived every turn that I had made in my floating mind.

We went for food in the huge basement restaurant filled with hundreds of skiers, and I was undoubtedly the only snowboarder. I noticed a rowdy bunch of British skiers in their twenties becoming very boisterous and drunk. I saw one of them pull a bewildered stray cat out of his coat and let it go. The cat ran and they chased it screaming, as if it had suddenly appeared, in a scene that would have been more at home in a Marx Brothers movie. The cat ran under the huge buffet tablecloth and they dived across the floor after it. The cloth slid off with a huge clattering of hot food and dishes. The waiters ran around in confusion and caused a wall of laughter across the restaurant. When the uproar finally calmed down and went quiet, two of the group stood up some yards apart. One shouted out, 'I am going to turn this piece of bread into toast.' Hundreds watched in disbelief. The other one spat a mouth full of petrol at the bread and lit it! Whoof. The flame was huge and licked across the heads of some seated guests. The waiters instantly ran towards them to prevent anymore ensuing chaos and a scuffle broke out. The situation no longer seemed funny as there were families with young children and the atmosphere had definitely changed for the worse.

The furore continued afterwards in the bar. We later heard that the Andorran police had become involved and one of the skiers allegedly hit one of the policemen and was consequently dumped at the border with next to nothing in the freezing night! The hotel was much quieter after that. In later years, when snowboarders were criticised for their behaviour, I would recall my early introduction to badly behaved skiers!

I continued the next day where I had left off, although the snow had now changed. It was icy and hard, more like some home grown Brecon days that we had encountered. I was rapidly learning something new every day, but not always something good. I repeated my gulley riding all day applying more and more pressure to the turns as I was going faster. This meant that my foot was rubbing up and down inside my boot, and unbeknown to me I had been graced with smaller than normal heels and feet, which would haunt me through many years of snowboarding. Consequently a large blister appeared on my heel by lunchtime but I had become oblivious to it. The pain eventually forced me to inspect it on a coffee break outside the restaurant, but I decided that it was fine and carried on regardless.

The next morning the big blister had broken and gone sceptic, and it was very painful to walk on. I went for medical help and was sent up the waterfalls to see a resident doctor on the slope. He took one look at it and tutted, while rubbing eye-watering stuff on it that sent me through the roof. He looked at my moon boots and wagged his finger at me, 'No moon boots!' he exclaimed. It was as much English as he had said, and as I left, as if to show his expertise he said, 'No moon boots!' I now had to sit around in the hotel in socks and it was purgatory, I had paid to be here in the mountains but I was grounded.

A few days later I returned to see the doctor wearing my only warm shoes as it was freezing. I walked in and he looked at my moon boots. 'No moon boots!' he exclaimed. Then he pointed to my foot and made a cutting motion. 'Off!' he said. I got the message but despite my ignorance he hadn't seen me in socks all day. This was serious, but in spite of his attitude he thankfully got me back on the slope for the last day. And what a day it was.

In the morning I peered out of the hotel window at the monsoon rain coming down through my blurry hung-over eyes. My partner rushed out fully kitted up, shouting, 'That will be snow at the top!' I couldn't muster any enthusiasm, so I followed an hour later after breakfast and several coffees. On reaching the slopes, I found masses of fresh fluffy powder; he was right that the heavy rain in the valley had created perfect snow at the top. Every turn was soft on my feet and I was floating down the mountain at breakneck speed. The gulley had become a soft fluffy dream now, but still few skiers had bothered to come out. This feeling of floating around on the mountain in three dimensions was very similar to that of surfing on a windless, glassy ocean. It was even better than the high I had got from watching that life-changing video all those years ago. I had reached an even higher state of charged emotions than I had ever expected in my wildest dreams. The hours of dedication and pain to get here was suddenly nothing. I had persevered, not really knowing how good this was going to feel. So, by the end of that magic day, my legs ran out of energy, and I took that crazy lift down the cliff for the last time, a very happy man.

On the long coach ride to the airport, the next day, I reflected on this strange first trip to a ski resort. I had learned so much in so many areas. I gave up riding in mountain boots and wearing moon boots from then on. I also knew that some skier's behaviour was as bad as any snowboarders. While on the slopes I had only seen two other snowboarders; one riding a Burton Elite snowboard, a developed extension of the toy Snurfer really, but he kept going round in circles. The reason being the board was far too short and the back foot was on the tail causing the board to pivot. He was struggling to learn like I had, and I wanted to help him but I was on a mission. The other snowboarder was like me. We immediately connected and we pulled up for a chat. Using my broken Spanish and his broken English we communicated, but what we really had in common were the boards, then without much ado we shook hands and rode off. I suddenly realised there was the same natural feeling between early boarders as the early surfers had discovered. We were like alternative aliens!

Within weeks of returning home, Keith and I hiked on an epic trip to a distant snowy ridge in the Beacons. We fought our way through peaty bogs and bracken and finally ascended a difficult steep face. On reaching the top, we were rewarded with amazing views over the hills to Mid Wales. We soon found some rideable snow and as I took off on my descent my experience in Andorra paid off with my ability to turn smoothly and quickly. My friend Keith was amazed and still at the stage I had been at, but being as he was I knew it wouldn't last long.

Hearts beating and feet squidging on our way back to the car, Keith blurted out, 'Right then, let's book a trip to the Alps before the end of the season.'

Consequently a large group of skiers, the wife and daughter, and three boarders arrived in Val d'Isere and Tignes glacier in April. It was hot and sunny and there was snow everywhere. The women were able to sunbathe at lunchtimes and we rode in t-shirts. It was an amazing summer-winter holiday capped off with blue skies every day. Chow provided us with the evening comedy, even while using broomsticks as crutches after twisting his knee. And I bought soft comfy Sorrel boots to alleviate the pain from the first trip. There were shops with snowboards for sale and t-shirts with snowboarders on that had suddenly appeared. It was happening!

We met some local boarders who were jumping off the snow bank against the restaurant terrace. They did this while we were sat on the terrace with our beer and chips watching them pass by our heads. We then chatted to them, as there still weren't many snowboarders in the resort. Immediately following their departure, Keith's windsurfing skills rose to the surface and within minutes he was successfully copying their jumps. I had been left behind him again!

My Sims board and I became more and more connected, and I was now comfortably pushing myself down steeper and steeper slopes and slipping off the edge of the marked pistes into natural terrain. A strong bond developed between us as we travelled many miles together that week. I now understood how Huw had done such great stuff on this board, despite having to bend the camber back into the board each night; it was a flyer! From that moment on, I knew that our homemade boards were finished and coincidently, Keith was encountering problems with the surf factory partnership and he wanted out. After our return home, Keith faded from the snowboarding scene upon entry to college, but never gave up pushing the boundaries in mountain biking, kite surfing and whatever came along.

CHAPTER NINE — 1988 to 1989

— THE BRITISH ISLES —

'Something and Nothing.' —
the south-westerly wind shouts and whispers

The summer of '88 was spent daydreaming of snowboarding, while working and surfing the infrequent summer swells. In that summer an artificial ski slope had opened in Pembrey Country Park, about half an hour's drive away. So with much apprehension, I decided to revisit one of these slopes of pain, or should I say a desiccated incline. I approached the slope with a different attitude to my previous experience, and this time I started near the bottom and worked my way up. I traversed the slope carefully and worked out how the board reacted to the slope, and after half an hour I had cracked the turns.

I was now ready for the quirky lift, and my creaky knee winced in anticipation, before the friendly staff there gave me some tips. Apprehensively, I waited at the bottom and hurriedly put the shiny pole between my legs and took off shakily to the top. Everything was easier now that I had been to a real resort, and I was quickly jumping off the little plateaus in the slope, and enjoying flying through the air. A couple of minor wipe outs kept me in check, but I was now happy with the artificial surface, and on a positive note this meant that I could practice all year! I was buzzing after a session on a plastic hill, but it still wasn't like the real thing.

I became a regular on the Pembrey slope, and as a result began to ride it competently, even though I was an object of curiosity for the local skiers. The usual comment that I would receive would be, 'That looks difficult,' and eventually skiers would stop me and ask how I had learned this new sport, and whether they could have a go? The manager of the slope was really approachable and encouraging, so we worked out how I could break down the riding process into learning stages.

Then, without further ado, I started teaching the occasional skier. It was hard at first, but I applied my own long learning curve of mistakes. For safety reasons I padded the beginners to reduce the risks, clearly taken directly from my own diary of pain. I abandoned my own board so that I could support them whilst they learnt the basic manoeuvres, and I only had one board anyway! I practiced the learning stages myself to be familiar with their difficulties, and what started as a trickle of interest steadily increased to the point where I began to need more boards.

Sunday afternoons were to be avoided for teaching, the reason being that the slope was surrounded by rural farming communities and attracted many youngsters. They tended to go to the top and fly straight down with reckless abandon to the cheering of their mates; it was truly *Ski Sunday*. The biggest wipeout got the biggest cheer and it became more like a missile range rather than a ski slope, but it was good business for the local A & E. I used to enjoy watching the crazy antics though. Then after a few months some of the staff had learned to board with me and we now had a fun group headed by the witty raconteur Neville Davies. A loosely knit fun scene began to develop, and in the dark winter evenings the sessions riding together burst with exuberance.

By now I was intrigued to find out what was going on in other parts of the British Isles. I had felt a bit isolated in my teaching experience at Pembrey and was unsure what was happening elsewhere. I remembered that my friend Huw Parsons had driven to Scotland to compete in the first British Championships on snow. He had also driven to the Alps to the first world competition to be held in Europe, so there was a developing scene out there somewhere. Although he had not taken competition too seriously, his competitive nature ensured that he always put his best performance in, and Huw had witnessed the level of other riders from other parts of the world, using the competitions to have some social fun. He had made contact with the other rising snowboarders of the world.

Unbeknown to me, in North Wales a similar story was taking place centred around Tudor Thomas, or 'Chod' as he was known. Chod had seen adverts for

Sims snowboards in American skate mags and had tried with varying success to make one out of a ski. When it snowed locally he had tried to ride it and then he had seen my brief news slot on the BBC, he was amazed that someone else had made a board. He made enquiries and he was then on the same well-beaten path to Outdoor Action. His journey to the Mecca of snowboarding had taken four hours by train in order for him to witness a real snowboard for the first time, just like I had! In typical Welsh style he then caught the train back home without buying anything.

Bizarrely, Chod's dad was a partner in the Llandudno ski slope but had banned his own son from ever defiling the sacred ski slope with a snowboard. When Chod finally got his hands on a new Sims blade, bought from Shiner, the infamous skateboard importer, he had to sneak on to the abrasive slope in the dark. While learning in the pitch black he clearly wiped out a lot. So there were pockets of curious snowboarders, as crazy as I was suddenly appearing around the country, sparked off by something as simple as a picture in a magazine.

It took a lot of phone calls in those pre-Internet days to find out what was going on though, as there was no easy information path at this time. From these calls it appeared that there was a newly-formed snowboard association, but surrounded in mystery and intrigue, but there again reality never ceased to surprise me.

I had heard a rumour that a Glaswegian skate

park based in a church called 'The Angel Lights,' had something to do with it. After quite a few attempts, I finally managed to speak to someone there called Paul Welsh. A strange conversation ensued as he seemed almost reticent about my questions, as if it was all top secret. The outcome of the call was that I had discovered a loosely held together snowboard association, and an idea was afoot to hold the first British Dry slope Championships. Sheffield Ski slope was the chosen venue as it was centrally placed in the UK, and mid-summer the chosen time, and I saw this as my opportunity to meet up with other boarders. However, this vague competition was a long way off and I had plenty going on already in my busy life.

It later transpired that a few 'heads' in Scotland and England had got together and put forward the idea of a British Championships at Sheffield Ski slope. The aforementioned Paul Welsh, along with Jeremy Sladen from Nottingham and Dave Furneau from Rugby were definitely party to this seed. Although Paul and Angel Lights had started an informal association the others thought that there should be a more official body. One that would be correctly run and with proper links to the rest of the snowboarding world, not one menaced with dark undertones.

Jeremy Sladen had tasted snowboarding while on a skiing holiday in the Pyrenees with his wife in 1984. Skiing was not really his thing so he had rented out a French made 'powder' type board along with the ubiquitous moon boots and straps as bindings. Although not the most successful of experiences, somewhere deep down he knew that he would go back to it one day. When he moved from Nottingham to Glasgow he had heard that the Angel Lights Church skaters had taken trips to the Scottish ski resorts to snowboard, and Jeremy decided to go along with them.

Dave Furneau had started snowboarding around 1985 in snowy hills around Rugby. His skater friend Mon Barbour had butchered a plastic sled and fitted a rope to the nose like a Snurfer. That was the start of a love affair with snowboarding, and Dave was a good all round skater and regularly met up with other skaters like Rob Needham, Martin Drayton and Ian Cocking at various downhill and slalom skate events. In particular, the Brands Hatch slalom skateboard events sparked a new movement of pioneers. They were all interested in this new way of riding the snow, and were to become early riders and a dynamic force in the development of British snowboarding.

These early organisers were going to bring together the unknown snowboarders that were randomly developing around the country.

Just like in the USA, the UK had misty beginnings to snowboarding, for years kids had stood on trays, plastic signs or sleds and had gone down the snow in imitation of surfing. Some surfers had attempted to ride surfboards in snow, and some skaters had tried the same ideas on skateboard decks many years prior to 'real' snowboards. Although there have been many claims to being early pioneers most ended up in a heap at the bottom of the hill.

However, the significant thing for me about the early days of snowboarding in the UK was not so much who had ridden a 'board.' But more importantly, who had stood up and helped to gel this new way of riding the mountain and plastic slopes that we made do with? These people would subsequently evolve the culture, which like all powerful movements would grow out of nothing. A network of boarders that sprung up and eventually formed a web across the UK, some just rode for fun, some for competition and some to evolve the organisation of the sport. Communication, in this pre-Internet era, was a very different game and so much more difficult and haphazard than it is now.

Obviously the new importers of boards wanted to make sales, and it served their interests to be a useful part of the network. Jeremy took a job with the Sims importer, which placed him right in the thick of it, and he had managed this by meeting the next Sims importer, Rodney George. Rodney was based in the Scottish Highlands and sold lobsters and shellfish for a living, but he had quickly become one of those early mysterious figures in our development, and had a big impact on the embryonic expanding snowboarding scene there.

Importers of snowboards became influential figures in the development of the British scene in a symbiotic relationship that could sometimes be positive, but edgy and difficult at other times. The snowboard lifestyle of sponsored riders could enhance or destroy the image of a brand, and if the brands credibility went out the window they could lose sales rapidly. Along with this brand wars had started almost immediately in the UK, and the importers had to fight their corner.

The importers sold to shops as they mushroomed, or to existing outdoor sports outlets. This allowed new snowboarders access to the snowboard lifestyle, just like I had gone to Huw's shop to learn more some years earlier. Snowboard only shops had more credibility amongst boarders, but selling skateboards added to the kudos, as the early anti-snowboard skaters attitude of California had mellowed. Skateboarding had peaked a decade or so ago, but was now ready for a resurgence. The vertical ramps used by skateboarders were on the wane, and the new street skating was now beginning to develop alongside snowboarding.

Next came the magazines, probably the most influential of all aspects on the scene. And the UK was blessed with some sharp-witted, hard-hitting paper fanzines, followed later by the glossy, irreverent, wonderful *SUK* (*Snowboard UK*). Homegrown random products like *Cheesegrater*, *International Loonies*, *Borderline*, *Oh for the smell of it*, *Damp Patch* and *Hyperactive* began to spring up. These were like the *Private Eye* for skaters and snowboarders. Once these started there was no stopping their influence on the snowboard scene and much easier access for neophytes.

The need for contests to bring together riders and the trade now existed, but this obviously resulted in winners and losers. Riders could get sponsored, board makers could get recognised, advancements in technology could be evolved and at the same time heroes were made. The magazines needed contests to promote sales, and although there was a pivotal role for contests in the scene, it also had its downsides. Soul boarders and snow anarchists saw little need for contests in snowboarding, especially in the same vein as skiing had developed. Therefore flouting the establishment was a part of the quickly developing culture, but in spite of this divided culture the first national big competition at Sheffield was vital in the development of the enigmatic soul of British snowboarding.

As ever, we looked across the pond to see what the American magazines were covering, *International Snowboard Magazine* and *Transworld Snowboarding* continued to feed our imaginations. These magazines had started in the mid-eighties and gave youngsters a window on this new world, and from then on the early heroes were created. It also lead to mainstream media portraying the lifestyle in a rebellious stereotypical way, and the magazines influence was to drive the future of British boarding like an unstoppable undercurrent. We also had the additional impact of central Europeans, who in spite of being generally more ski influenced, had their own early pioneers.

In France snowboarding was kick started by the iconic 1983 film *Apocalypse Snow*. A blend of crazy script, plus extreme riding for its time, and fantastic snow conditions, made this film a big hit in alternative sports circles. I wore my own video copy of the film out, and this film single-handedly managed to turn the Alps on to snowboarding and was continuously shown in many alpine bars throughout the Eighties. It was rumoured that the script was written after the creators had drunk a lot of red wine. The hero of the film, Regis Roland, rode a Winterstick swallowtail powder board whilst being pursued by baddies on mono skis, and managed to amaze the viewers with incredible tricks. It was filmed around the Les Arcs region in the Tarentaise Valley. Prior to the film being made in 1981, two of the American Winterstick team were invited to Les Arcs to demonstrate snowboarding, which probably set the scene for evolution in this area. The Europeans later took to the racing aspect of snowboarding slightly more though. Here we became sandwiched between the States and Europe, both with very differing attitudes and influences. Sounds familiar *n'est-ce pas*.

Not to be forgotten, or underestimated in its influence on the British scene, was that far northern area of the Isles, the only true snow ski resorts were situated in Scotland. Most are in the large Cairngorms National Park, further north than the two main cities of Scotland, Glasgow and Edinburgh, and they were home to many championships over the years. A hardcore group of boarders evolved there, but being so far north reduced their impact on the overall scene. A week in Scotland or a week in the Alps was a no-brainer for most boarders.

These resorts being smaller and lower than most alpine or North American ones stand at about 1200 metres. They also suffer from extreme weather in the form of high winds, sideways sleet and sudden warming. They are in the path of many moist winter low-pressure systems that charge across the Atlantic, but on the occasional blue-sky powder day they are as good as anywhere in the world. They are serious enough though to suffer avalanches, cornices and sadly, regular deaths often of mountain climbers and other unfortunates. Whichever way you look at it they are a big step up from my home turf, the Brecon Beacons.

Therefore at this early stage in UK snowboarding history there were already a myriad of influences taking place and growing simultaneously across the country. I had come to realise that the picture was way bigger than my little world, and there were a lot of little enclaves of individuals or groups located around the country. Although we were not yet connected up, we were ready to form a giant zorb.

— MIND BOMB —

'Snowboarding is not for sheep!' — Scottish crew

'Should I stay or should I go?' was the question that dominated my thinking in early January of 1989. As, without much notice, the first British Snowboard 'Training Camp' was announced, and this was the start to an explosive year.

In America the watershed between backcountry pioneer riders, and the more commercial spread of snowboarding to resorts and a bigger audience began to happen in the early '80s. In the UK the watershed year was 1989 as a slow motion explosion of events, combined with a new generation of boarders, evolved. The original seeds of us 'soul' boarders were about to be swamped by a new wave of media generated commercialism, and I still personally believe that the pre-1989 snowboarders of the UK were the original avant-garde trailblazers of snowboarding. They dabbled with boards, equipment and new techniques in a never-ending sea of optimism, and because of this unlimited perspective there was no fixed vision of what snowboarding was and where it was going. Fun and adventure were the motivational forces along with the chance to explore a totally new world.

The attraction for the post-1989 boarders was an alternative, dangerous, different, anti-establishment, colourful and addictive fun pastime. This image also neatly dovetailed with the cultural rave movement also happening in the underground musical scene at the time, with mutations of acid house, techno etc. This led to a visible crossover between surf/skate/BMX and any alternative sport or lifestyle around. Magazines, newspapers and videos often portrayed snowboarding in dramatic surroundings, and even the latest James Bond film had Roger Moore sliding down the mountain (even though we knew that it was Tom Sims). In conjunction with this media shift, Burton and Sims were selling thousands of boards and big business had quickly seen a new opportunity in a new worldwide market. In an attempt to make it look more attractive than it actually was predictions for the growth of the sport were wildly optimistic in the States, resulting in many financially burnt fingers soon to come!

I had found out from a poster in Outdoor Action that the first British snowboard camp was set for the 13th January 1989. For me to take this sudden opportunity, it was going to be a balance of finance, work and the wife's permission. After wrangling it through, I was given the green light. So I booked on the trip a little apprehensively. My biggest concerns were whether it would be good value for my hard earned money and my doubts about the camp being hosted by a ski company called 'Just Ski', hardly a great name for a snowboard camp!

I rang the O'Neill clothing company to try and scam some apparel, and they kindly donated a new snow jacket in black, purple, orange and blue. It was too big but it was my first bit of proper snow clothing. I then bought cheap tight-fitting blue C&A ski pants, which combined with the big jacket made me look more like a frog than an athlete, but I thought that I looked cool.

The day finally arrived and we took off by coach from London. It was hard to contain our excitement and great to chat to other boarders, mainly London boys like Mark Tebbenham and in particular with Phil Young, a likeable skater and music connoisseur from London. His first experience with a snowboard had come about a few years earlier, in extremely challenging circumstances. His friend Darren Robinson was working part-time for Faze 7, the skate importers, and they had spent hours drooling over a French magazine displaying a picture of a rider floating through powder. The article also showed how to make your own board. Fascinated and intrigued by this newfangled concept they decided to make plywood boards covered in bright graphics. They overcame the binding problem by drilling roller skate boots on to the top and had then, with unbelievable optimism, taken them on a school trip to Courmayeur.

On arriving in the resort situated on the slopes of Mount Blanc, they immediately took the highest lift straight to the summit. Phil put his board down on to the snow at the top and it started going down without him. After a comical scene in which he chased after it, eventually catching it in a gulley, they attempted to ride down the steep terrain. Initial trauma over they were hanging in by riding in survival mode, but upon successfully reaching the bottom of the forgiving powder slope Phil and Darren decided that this would become their lifetime mission! That is despite the fact that one roller boot had ripped out of the board on the way down.

Meanwhile, back on the bus, after many endless hours of rumbling conversation we finally ran out of things to say, and as the cheap bus seating was so uncomfortable it was a disturbed difficult sleep. A long night ensued as the coach sped across the dark vineyards of France finally depositing us in Serre Chevalier, completely exhausted.

We stayed in a rustic hotel in Serre Chevalier called 'Le Lievre Blanc' or 'The White Hare' en Anglais, a log fire and hot coffee helped the recovery process, but I was already beginning to fear the return trip!

This quaint old inn had become another meeting place for future snowboarders in the British scene. Martin Drayton was running the camp, and the two of us would go on to work together for some years. A then unknown photographer, Sang Tan, was seated by the big log fire along with Clive Boden, a London professional photographer (who just happened to have a summerhouse nearby my home). He had written a book on windsurfing and we soon became good friends. Sang was very interested in action photography and would go on to document much of the flourishing British snowboard scene. He would reliably attend as many of the events that he could, and like any good photographer had an invisible presence. His quiet unassuming manner gained him the respect of everyone. With increasing envy I learned that these two had the financial means to fly out and therefore avoid the endless coach journey that was awaiting me.

Jonno Gibbins was there too, and became a top competitor and an integral part of the British scene, and along with the aforementioned Phil Young this was bound to be a fun trip, whatever happened. There was a good atmosphere amongst us all, except for the 'so called' mountain experts, as this was the worst snowfall year in Alpine history for some time. A large high-pressure weather system lay over Europe and refused to budge, and in those pre-Internet days it wasn't easy to find out the expected snow conditions for the Alps. Looking across the trickling river all that we could see were large expanses of green grass and trees. There had been one steep ribbon of snow further along, but this looked precariously seriously steep to any novice, and the general consensus was that conditions were atrocious.

After too much wine and the resulting long, long sleep, we awoke to blue skies and more green grass, more food and more coffee. After collecting our kit we were transported to the lift pass office and given our weeks pass, and then taken to that dangerous looking steep run with artificial snow on it. Going up the lift we could see just how bad it was and totally beyond redemption. A much flatter run was open over the first ridge, but not much else, except for that awful steep descent. We got as high as we could and started to ride down, and it quickly became apparent who was who in the pecking order. Jonno instantly stood out from the rest, and even though my abilities were not quite able to match his, I rode quite well until we hit the steep descent that was for serious race skiers. One turn too fast in the slush and ice flipped me onto my back and I sped upside down endlessly for the rest of the run, just like a flapping turtle! I could easily have hit a rock or tree as I blindly slid out of control, damn right in front of everyone too!

It was clear by the evening that this situation was not acceptable to the 'clientele.' The ski company manager had agreed to transport us to two other resorts with glaciers, *Alp d'huex* and *Les Deux Alpes*. We had to pay for more lift passes, as the management of Serre Chevalier would not refund ours, the one awful run being open was their excuse not to refund us. This stuck in my throat and I decided that I would never come back; I vowed that they would pay for it in the long term.

The drive to the other resorts was a kaleidoscope of some of natures' finest scenery, but after a hundred hairpins in a coach driven by a crazy Frenchman we all felt enough was enough. We habitually passed little old mountain villages, one called *La Grave* had caught my attention, I looked out at this severe, steep mountain and wondered where anyone could ride on it; not knowing that in later years I would come to call it one of my spiritual homes and loves of my life.

Once on the glaciers we finally had space to ride in the glorious sunshine, and by the time that we travelled there we missed the cold, morning boilerplate ice. Instead, we were able to enjoy the soft spring snow that the sun had conveniently warmed up for us. Martin rode competently and showed us some useful tips, such as the 'in' riding style, which at that time was to tuck your back knee into the front knee. This didn't work well for me as it caused sharp pain in my injured knee, and the technique was more popular with the alpine riders of Europe. Europeans at that time did not have the surf and skate backgrounds of West coast America; they were more into wearing hard ski mountaineering boots, hard bindings and race boards. The board shapes were developing much narrower and had the feet angled steeply towards the front rather than flat across the board in a true surfer style. The resulting riding position was far more exaggerated than had been between Sims freestyle boards and Burton's racier boards. Europe was on a mission to perfect racing snowboards, however the UK had more freestyle riders than racers, and we considered ourselves more like the USA. Surfers and skaters stood on their boards with a much flatter foot stance, but some of us did become AC/DC.

After a few days, Martin wiped out badly and injured his leg, so a local French boarder was hired to take us out. Martin had already said that Jonno Gibbins and myself had arrived at his level already, so a new instructor suited us. Martin had taken a different route into our pursuit by purchasing a Winterstick snowboard and booking trips to the Alps to sketchily learn to ride it. On his second trip he decided to follow two boarders off-piste, only to lose them and ride straight off a hidden cliff. He luckily fell into deep snow and had to be dug out by soldiers on avalanche training! Despite the lack of many new techniques gained, we all pushed each other along and our riding skills definitely improved. One surprise that I did discover was that Jonno's board was one of the Sims Blades I had seen opened in Huw's shop some time ago; his was one of the six Sims boards ordered for the UK that year. Jonno's previous summer had been spent working in the French Alps in the resort of Tignes as a dishwasher. This meant that he rode the glacier in the mornings, before work, and consequently his riding improved quickly, especially with this new Sims board.

As with many of us, he had come to this new snowboarding lifestyle in a strange way as he had gone to Australia on a working holiday after leaving school, and he had quickly secured an unlikely job as a ski technician in Mt Buller ski resort. He had thought he was applying for a water skiing job and wasn't aware that there was any snow in Oz. Finding himself immersed in an alien world he adapted quickly and soon hung out with an English lad who told him about snowboarding. With their hard earned cash they went and bought Sims Fe 140 boards and Sorrel walking boots, only to find out that snowboarding was banned in Mt Buller! As a result they moved to Falls Creek and Jonno got a job as a chalet 'girl,' and within a few weeks of learning to board Jonno successfully entered the Aussie National Championships, achieving a position of thirteenth! Then on his return to the UK he had bought a Sims Blade from Outdoor Action in Cardiff and whilst looking around the shop saw the poster for the first Just Ski Camp. So bingo here he was, and the two of us were in awe of the new Sims Blade, which was a huge leap in the latest board technology.

I began to follow Jonno like a sheepdog so that I could prise more knowledge from him. I watched how he went from edge to edge with tremendous speed. When I tried to replicate his style I would manage several quick turns and then unexpectedly catch an edge in the snow and get dusted. I was slowly improving by the 'no pain no gain' method again, but with every small success the pain was soon forgotten, and after a long shower we were ready for the evening. We all bonded well and enjoyed discussing the day's adventures by the log fire with a glass of wine or two. Good French cuisine and a crackling fire made up for the appalling snow conditions. Overall it was a good week sandwiched between two horrible journeys. More importantly, new connections had been made, and the British scene, after this inaugural Just Ski snowboard camp, had more fanatical followers joining the band. These invisible tentacles would gradually begin to creep around the UK like snow triffids.

On my return home I managed to combine teaching at Pembrey and working my day job. Although I knew that there was to be a second British Championships on real snow on the 10th March 1989, at Glenshee, I did not have the time or the finances to enter. The paper fanzine 'Hyper Active' was the thrown together mouthpiece of the Scottish Association of Snowboarding. In the third issue of Hyper Active there was a write up for the event by Stephen Crampton, and it also had an article in the 'magazine' that I had put together for them entitled 'Shredding Dendix'. At that time there were quite a few dry slopes scattered around Scotland, and strangely, one I was invited to many years later was inside Faslane, the nuclear submarine base! However, the Hyper Active crew kindly posted me their magazine to keep me in touch with snowboarding life in Scotland at the massive expense of a beer or two.

Three weeks prior to this second British Championships there was no snow, then suddenly a huge fall of snow descended, but problems arose when the temperatures gradually crept up. By the day of the contest the snow was poor and sketchy for the contest. However there was a blue sky. The event had been sponsored by The Sun newspaper along with Glasgow shop '7th Wave' and this had proved that media interest was really starting to grow, despite the resistance of the traditional skiing fraternity. The Scottish lads put on a good show holding a slalom race in icy conditions, and then a freestyle event, but they could not build a halfpipe due to the continued lack of snow so used hand shovels to build jumps instead.

One of the competitors became a great asset to British boarding, Noel Gaddo, a.k.a. the 'Flying Dutchman' who was of Dutch descent, but who had spent a lot of his time competing and training in Austria. He had a solid physique and was a self-described 'butch' snowboarder who loved speed and air. His boarding career had started around 1985 and he was now pivotal in the Scottish scene development, and instrumental in the black and white paper magazine Hyper Active. Based in Aberdeen, he would often appear in many of the British events, sharing with us his valuable knowledge, and his fun chameleon like character made him a firm favourite in different countries.

At the Scottish event he easily won the slalom and came second overall, and it was quite evident that his snowboarding technique was streets ahead, and in the ensuing years all further snowboard competitions would be deemed 'open' in order to allow Noel to compete! He was our guide and mascot in many ways.

Stuart Duncan won the overall competition by placing first in the freestyle. Jonno Gibbins, after making the long trip from France and the recent Just

Ski camp, came sixth overall, and the Scottish lads did very well on their home patch, but we did not as yet have any women competing in our events. At this stage it was mainly a male only thing to shred the mountains, but it was also a time when the standard of riding varied immensely. The event was fun for this very reason but it also helped to motivate riders to improve. A slim wedge of serious competition was beginning to evolve, although so too was the anti-establishment and the movement against pre-ordained skiing attitudes. Snowboarding had already attracted a complex mix of individuals, and it was easy to understand how these differing attitudes were surfacing. I understood how competition helped development, but that side of snowboarding didn't particularly apply to myself. Although I was curious as to where this new found competitive spirit would lead the sport, I was still hopeful that my rush of riding down the mountain, as a mountain surfer, would not become just another mainstream commercial sports system. The fun side of snowboarding was precious and I soon realised could very easily be lost in the drive for competitive advancement.

This was also the year I found out that a British snowboard company had set up a workshop near Laggan, in the Highlands. Although there had been several early attempts at making boards, like our 'Snow Shark', this was a proper board with ash wood cores, P-tex bases, sidewalls and metal edges. Al Fleming and Gus Gillard were producing boards under the name 'Acid Snow.' The models they made were named after philosophers and scientists, like the appropriately named Max Planck!

The boards worked well, and the dynamic duo with a deep knowledge of how a snowboard really worked, also knew how to have a good time. Their legendary parties in an isolated farmhouse in Laggan were a part of early snowboarding folklore, especially as the parties were partly sponsored by their Highland grant money. They were well respected by everyone, and their opinion of snowboarding was that it should be fun first, and that competition was a minor part. To prove this they sponsored early boarder, Rob Needham, renowned for his head on skateboard approach, but for Rob results were secondary to having a crazy session. Acid Snow had the early snowboard roots as their philosophy, with a very unique British twist, and as a result went on to survive for many seasons, but like many other home grown products would inevitably succumb to cheaper foreign imports.

Another event also took place at this time, which opened doors for new boarders, and became known as the 'Burton Tour.' When Huw and Lyndsey at the Outdoor Action shop didn't take the option to import Burton boards, mainly due to the expense involved, the opportunity was eventually grabbed by Second Level Sport Ltd. Jake Burton, the American CEO of Burton boards, had his own personal vision for snowboard design, and despite some early failures he soon learned from his mistakes. His persistence and vision began to shine through, and every little criticism or annoyance with the Burton boards was considered and soon added to next year's development plan. It was a rolling development process based on feedback from his riders, who coincidentally were butchering his new equipment, but only to suit their own needs. Jake's business background and commitment would blaze a trail over the next decade, and he committed to a tour of the UK using good riders to demonstrate the sport on dry slopes. Beginners were allowed to try a board under a 'controlled' situation and the general feedback was good, and a party atmosphere was created, and once again it brought together many new riders.

The Burton tour covered around thirty slopes across the UK, including the Sheffield competition and the British Ski Show. The Swatch company joined in to promote their trendy watches, and it successfully ran from June until November. The riders involved in promoting the boards were Stuart Duncan, Noel Gaddo, Dave Furneau, Martin Drayton and Paul Turner. Local riders were drawn in and recently appointed Nick Boothroyd oversaw the events whilst failing to keep some form of control over some of the riders! This tour firmly put Burton on the map and created many new devotees to the brand, but despite the campaign actual board sales remained low, and by the end of 1989 there were less than a thousand snowboarders in the UK, and even more board manufacturers were starting up in the

U.S. and Europe. A bewildering array of names appeared on the scene very quickly, and further to those already mentioned, there were the following: Avalanche, Barfoot, Hooger Booger, Funky, Crystal Ocean, Gnu, Kemper, Snowtect, Santa Cruz, G&S, Nitro, Jacks, Hot, Dominator, Checker Pig, Winter Surf, Gaspo, Nidecker, Crazy Banana, Black Snow, Look, K2, Elan, Mistral, F2, Fanatic and maybe more. This meant that in 1989 almost anyone who competed could find a company to sponsor them with a board! The same imbalance had occurred in America, especially with the excessive prize money on offer there. The hype and media image was causing a prolapse in the actual picture.

As deep as I was being drawn into the complex world of snowboarding, I was still living and working in Swansea. So, as each summer ends and like all British surfers I was preparing for the predictable autumn storms, however, that was prior to the unpredictable climate change era. On time, a huge low pressure piled in after summer and sent massive messy waves up the Bristol Channel, turning the ocean into an unorchestrated hell. On a pushing tide these unruly waves wrap around Oxwich Point and march into their own wind because of the contours of the shoreline funnelling the wind thus creating a natural phenomena. The east facing sheltered beach of Oxwich suddenly changes from a reliably serene flat bay, to a feast of hollow tubing waves. The very wind that makes them huge and messy in the Bristol Channel cleans them up and grooms them into respectable barrels in the bay, ideal for surfers to try and get inside them.

A few of us had driven there listening to a stern radio presenter warning people to take care of high winds and flooding; trees were shaking to their roots, and the road past the marshes was flooded. The violent wind rattled the car as we changed in the car park, and the wind nearly blew the doors off. Just walking down the beach with a surfboard was a challenge as it flipped backward and forwards like a demented see-saw hitting me on both sides of my body. Once in the relatively warm sea it was much easier, as I paddled out and waited outside of the impact zone. The grey clouds whipped along as I stared at the backs of huge waves further out in the channel heading east, and then it was time for the 'waiting in a storm' game.

The waves were suddenly rearing up into the air, as the wind would prevent them from breaking until the last second and simultaneously blowing the tops off in a long white stream of spray. I paddled for several potential waves but couldn't overcome the wind holding me back. Finally I got one and plummeted fast down the face. A sharp turn at the bottom put me in the almond eye of the wave, and a moment of intense beauty followed. I stood crouched and relaxed as the board sped along in the steep face and time seemed to stand still. This picture stuck in my mind forever, but the white water coming the other way put a sudden end to my slow-ocean dream as it took me out and under. Dreams were replaced by cold reality as the wetsuit was ripped wide open at the zip and cool water rushed in putting an end to my moment of triumph. It didn't matter as all I could do was laugh at this epic storm.

We spent a few hours in this pleasure zone, and at one point the clouds broke apart, the sun appeared as the small intense showers rushed by in their journey up the channel. From the chaos a perfect rainbow arched across the distant Three Cliffs beach as the sundry seabirds wheeled above the feeding fish. The spray off the tops of the waves created all the colours of the rainbow, surrounding us with moments of pure magic. However, while sat in this ocean of splendour my mind darted back to the forthcoming snowboard event in 'way up north' Sheffield, and the possibility of putting myself in an unknown stressful situation. What the hell was this Angel Lights thing, and did I really want to get more involved in snowboarding when I had all this on my own doorstep?

Anyway, just as curiosity killed the cat, humans need fresh pastures to explore, and I found myself being drawn into this exciting prospect of a huge snowboard event on plastic. I told myself surfing was becoming crowded out partly due to surf lessons for beginners combined with a new wave of Swansea University surfing students! I did not want to keep opening the same door, the first cracks in my love affair with surfing had appeared, and snowboarding had slowly become the new mistress.

So having finally convinced myself, I excitedly

left Swansea with a young lad that I had recently taught to snowboard, John Knight. We arrived at the ski slope in Sheffield after getting completely lost in the back streets, and the sight of what we saw shocked us. A vast array of Dendix artificial slopes were spread over a large ridge looking down on the city, a veritable plastic mountain in the sky. Apparently this was the biggest dry slope in Europe and had been opened in 1988, and with continual expansions in order to emulate a real ski resort. There were numerous runs, one even had a hollow compression midway, with bumps and banks, along with a freestyle section and excellent beginners area. It seemed that Sheffield could be dry slope heaven and hell for the riders. Here at the first big artificial event for snowboarding in the UK the wider roots of British snowboarding were being made. Soon the microscopic bubbles of British boarders began to join together.

The inaugural embryonic British Snowboard Association was in full swing and many of the riders were meeting their counterparts for the first time. Friendships and links developed from here and the progress of British snowboarding consequently moved onwards. Although it wasn't really obvious at the time, this event was key to the future of our snowboard scene, as most of the entrants were determined to stick around and become a part of this growing enfant terrible.

Behind the scenes there had been a lot of doubt,

faxes, financial juggling and bravado. Jeremy and Dave pushed the event along at the risk of their own financial loss. The importer for K2 was initially supportive, but went through personnel changes, and then withdrew their financial input. The cost of a marquee was thought to be too much, and the drafted prize money added up to a ridiculous amount. It was new territory and a huge learning curve consequently the final programme underwent constant change until finally forced by the clock into its endmost format. It was always going to be a fun amateur event, and perhaps that was its beauty, and obviously, as Jeremy had been involved the partying attitude took precedence over everything else. However, it could have been one expensive party for Jeremy and Dave if the sponsors had failed to finance the event, as neither of them were flushed with money at this time.

The importers of boards, who were rightly apprehensive at this first ever dry slope championships, involved at the time were Acid Snow, Sims, Burton, K2, Look, Mistral and Rossignol. Their sales of boards were low and their financial budgets tight for snowboarding. In addition, they also had to sponsor some riders with equipment, just to have a profile name. These companies needed to see a professionally run event as in the established ski contests, but this went totally against the snowboarding free spirit and approach to life. These companies and those with shareholders were worried about the image that snowboarding was portraying, due in part to some of the adverse stories that filtered back from the States, many of them justified.

The atmosphere on arrival at the site was very laid back; boarders were slightly tentative about meeting other unfamiliar boarders at first. We introduced ourselves to Paul Welsh, from Angel Lights, with his dark, curly Marc Bolan hairstyle, and somehow managed to get John registered in the competition mayhem. My own competition career was basically over after the cursed knee had blown up yet again after a wipe out at Pembrey slope. In the café I got to meet Jeremy and Dave, who were outwardly brimming with optimism and doing their best to chat to everyone. Jeremy seemed like a lovable rogue with an athletic tongue having multiple conversations at once, and Dave's face reflected the concern of the big risks being taken by their giant snowboard party, beneath his busy social exterior.

I climbed the huge slope and watched John practising on this impressive set up, but it was still Dendix, not real snow I told myself to ease my frustration. On a dry day, on a day like this, the friction between the matting and the descending board was high. As I watched, I could see John's board shuddering as it hit dry patches, and suddenly it would catch nearly throwing him over the nose. I could envisage problems on such a long slope with the inherent dangers of the matting design. I chatted to him about it thinking it may be better to keep the board on its edges more as this would increase his speed, but hopefully reduce this sudden drag.

Perhaps the most important point about this competition is that many years later the organisers and quite a few riders that I spoke to couldn't remember the results! It was not about winning so much as a great get together for the first time, and everyone was in a new situation and atmosphere. Also it was a fashion show of sorts to see what clothing and boards were being sported. Pink pants, some with leopard spots, psychedelic Tapis Volant one piece suits, block colours of Look and Jeremy's psychotic pants were all on display. Only the boys from Keith, in Scotland, pointed to the future with their dark 'No Worries' sponsored clothing.

There were some very good riders there who were great to watch, and during the session John met people in the lift queue and chatted happily. The freestyle event was visually exciting and some unexpected big airs and tricks were performed. Allan Innes and Rusty Russell were hitting the big ramp simultaneously like flying twins with the same sponsored clothing and boards. Flamboyant Dutchman Noel Gaddo stole the overall crown as 'Open Champion' with a blistering race technique and big airs.

The general atmosphere had improved immensely, that was until I went to talk to Paul Welsh again. This time I offered to assist with the organisation of the loose British Snowboard Association, as I knew there was a strong developing interest in the Swansea area. Stood behind him was a large bald person who hardly spoke, seeming to have some sort of influence over Paul. I picked up a strange vibe to say the least, as I offered my services only to be met with half-hearted approval. The shadowy guy just eyeballed me, and when asking Jeremy about him afterwards was told that 'Dorky' or the 'Dalai Balaclava,' as Jeremy called him was not in it for the good of the sport. I knew instantly that I wanted no further dealings with these characters. Jeremy and Dave had far better plans, and I decided to stick with them.

I later found out more about Angel Lights Planetary Skate Park in the after event party. It turned out to be a charity centred on a skate park in a church, in Anniesland, Glasgow. A few of the skaters said that it was linked to Bhagwan Shree Rajneesh, and the controversial Indian spiritual leader was famous for having ninety-three Rolls Royce's, amongst many other strange tales. Followers often gave up all their worldly possessions for him and it seemed that drugs, sex and violence were never far away from the hippy-dippy world that he represented, which I wanted no part of.

— CHANNEL VIEW —

*'Men use violence against women and
women steal men's souls.' – Ancient*

In the midst of a progressively busy snowboarding year, and while holding down my civil service job, we had coincidentally decided to move house! Probably not as newsworthy as the fall of the Berlin wall though, despite the spirit of the wall remaining in place.

We moved from quiet suburbia to a four-storey townhouse, which operated as a commercial guesthouse. It overlooked St Helens Rugby and Cricket ground, renowned for Sir Garfield Sobers hitting six sixes in one over, and was just two minutes from the sea when the tide was in! I could check the tide and swell from the big picture window in the living room, and also have the pleasure of watching the big games of rugby and cricket for free in the ground below.

My wife ran the business, and to start with we had mainly travelling contractors staying with us, so it was not a busy place at that time. Although a bunch of London-based, Scottish surfers soon found us, and began to come down for regular weekends of surfing and partying. They would take the opportunity to ply me with beer in the early evening, to find out where the Gower secret spots were, and then they would head out to town for 'a big night out.' Snowboarders would sometimes come and stay, which helped a little bit. However, one day a longhaired, good looking, student-type walked in the door and he used his cheeky, immediate charm to introduce himself as 'Dave Ward Smith.' He had attended Swansea University, but spent most of his time flying hang gliders around the hills of South Wales. He never seemed to wear shoes during the warmer months and exhibited a cool, casual outlook on life. He took up the new sport of Paragliding around 1986, and quickly started a teaching school after leaving university. When he discovered the laid back atmosphere of our guesthouse, he realised that his sports customers would feel right at home. Weekends would be booked up with his crazy kamikaze followers during the summer months, followed by even more serious pilots at other times of the year. I quickly nicknamed him 'The Flying Hippy,' and some of his crazy clients had connections with the numerous importers of sports goods. I used to imagine these commercial reps being ordered to go and learn to paraglide, just in case it went global!

Luckily, paragliding injuries were not as frequent as snowboarding, but they would often result in severe trauma or death! Dave had spent a lot of time perfecting his sport, and despite his laid back attitude was determined to make it as safe as possible. Importantly for me the contacts with various sports distributors were very useful for my own ambitions. I saw a similarity in most of these characters that were drawn in the first wave of this sport to the early snowboarders. One of these flyers came down from West Wales and described how he had built his own hang glider, out of bamboo and plastic… and flown it into the sea from a cliff, a bit different to building your own snowboard!

One of the visiting reps came from a company called Ultrasport, and John Dight brought with him some recently developed mountain bikes on one of these paragliding training excursions. So after a few drinks in the local pub he didn't have to ask me twice to try one, and we were soon whizzing around the Swansea cycle paths in the dark. They were a lot of fun, and I was hooked on another sport now, one that suited the gaps between surfing and snowboarding. They also imported Sims snowboards and Off-road bikes, and Johns' slick patter had me helping him to promote these brands.

I later went to the Alps with John, on a snowboarding, biking and flying trip and on this excursion to Val d'isere, we flew a paraglider into a deep snow-covered valley from a hill that had been easy to hike up. When I pointed out to John that there was 6 inches of stitching undone on the wing, he nonchalantly told me that he had been meaning to stitch it up for some time!

That same trip we hooked up with a sports photographer from Montana, Bob Allen. Bob wanted to take a mountain bike to the top of Le Fornet glacier and ride it all the way down. The French resort manager had no qualms about this, but said that we must make our attempt early. Unbelievably, we were chair lifted up before the masses appeared on the slopes, and I rode a snowboard and took photos on the way down. We also fixed the camera to the bike and did shots of us all going down the glacier. Fearlessly, Bob decided to try a straight run through a steep mogul field on his bike, and I took a shot of him cycling flat out through the bumps, with a manic grin on his bearded face. By now the throng of skiers were watching our antics in disbelief, and later that day in the *après* ski bar John made up a preposterous story to fit the photos, and bingo, we had an article. Thanks to Bob and John I had a centre page spread shot of Bob in the moguls, and I went on to cover more mountain bike articles for a few years.

At the guesthouse Dave had a habit of appearing suddenly in bare feet, with scruffy blond hair, and a pink flying jacket, his normal apparel. When he did this I would expect the unexpected, as he would sometimes arrive out of the blue in desperation. This time he was in urgent need of photos of his students learning to fly for a new brochure. He had seen some of my pictures of action sports on the walls, which impressed him greatly, and he knew he wouldn't be paying me any cash! In spite of this I accompanied them to Rhossili Downs, an incredible vista overlooking the five-mile stretch of sands that was my usual surfing beach. The downs were perfect for paragliding, as they comprised a west facing ridge providing an easy nursery slope for flying in west winds.

After shooting many rolls of film on a day like this with blue sky and no wind, I was suddenly terrified to hear the words 'your turn!' At this point in time I had never flown under a handkerchief before! I had picked up some knowledge about paragliding, but there was a big difference in sitting comfortably in the pub discussing high altitude flying to actually steeping off the cliff into the void.

All the beginners so far had flown out straight above the raised cliff, hundreds of feet below, and landed way out on the golden flat sand, this made for an easy first flight without turns. Once he got my take off sorted, I ran off the edge and instantly flew into a huge space of air that seemed like a black hole. It was instantaneously breathtaking and beautiful – serene even. Here it was that again that feeling; I was back in my floating world! Yet again my moment of serenity was about to be shattered, as unbeknown to Dave and myself, the sun was slowly heating up the exposed sand, resulting in bubbles of hot air rising quickly upwards. It was one of these early hot air thermals that lifted me up so violently that it felt like God had grabbed my collar. I was going up fast instead of down slow. Then just as quickly I outran the thermal diving into a patch of cooler sink! Now I was going down all right, plummeting to the earth at light speed. All that I can remember was a man walking his dog below me with a look of horror on his face at my predicament. Seconds later, I was rushing at the raised cliff below and yanked very hard on the two brake handles of the glider, just as it seemed inevitable that I would crash land. The air brakes worked thankfully, and I was briefly suspended a few feet above the ground, God's hand again had allowed me to gently step onto terra firma. Phew! Dave called off the beginners flying for the rest of the day due to these aggressive thermals.

After walking slowly back up to the top of the ridge, filled with adrenaline, I stood at the edge where I had taken off. I was eating a sandwich and reflecting on that wild experience while the breeze had picked up, unbeknown to me Dave took off yards behind me. He flew along just above the ground and swiped the sandwich out of my hand, as he made his escape into the blue, I shouted, 'You effing seagull, give me that back!' That was a typical day with the Flying Hippy, although, my first flight was hardly eventful compared to the one Dave once had, when his lines broke, and he fell one thousand feet into a tree and walked away unharmed. Half-man, half-bird.

So Channel View Guesthouse became a bustling place of like-minded adrenaline junkies and a hot bed of cultural and idealistic crossovers. It was interesting to see the conflict between the established hang gliders, and the new breed of paragliders. They flew at different speeds and took different paths, much like the skier and snowboard conflict. Good skiers tend to go down the fall line rapidly transferring weight edge to edge, wiggling their bums, while snowboarders take wider turns, so this inevitably results in a clash of styles and people on narrow pistes. Around this time the Scottish crew were referring to skiers as 'sheep,' while further south the snowboarders used the unflattering 'pricks on sticks,' the skiers retaliated with the classic 'gays on trays.'

Just as in America, the new blood brought fresh attitudes to the mountains, and boarders began to emulate the new stars across the pond, assimilating trends from skate and city cultures. Shaun Palmer in the US was winning contests and living the rock 'n' roll lifestyle, and swearing and drinking were *de rigeur*. It was great media stuff, and the conservative establishment of skiing became a target for snowboarders. They were an easy wind up for boarders, and they did themselves no favours with unfounded criticisms like 'they chop the snow up with their boards!' We didn't mind the criticism, as we felt justified and modern, carving a fun path through their pistes.

Besides Shaun Palmer, the US had the blond spiky haired Damian Sanders as a media figurehead. He was always photographed performing big airs in Day-Glo colours, looking entirely menacing. He rode and promoted his brothers boards named 'Avalanche,' but strangely, he rode with hard ski type boots and hard bindings. Although this was a controlled way to ride, this provided a contrast, as it was not the more common image of soft boots and freestyle that had found favour with the US. In Europe, the Alpine countries took to hard ski boots, and excelled on racing boards that enabled them to really carve fast powerful turns on firm pistes. A schism within the boarding world, which had started initially between Burton and Sims, was now an intercontinental controversy!

It became the trend in the Alpine countries to take hard boot carving off the piste, and two riders, Peter Bauer and Jean Nerva, were at the figurehead of this movement. They rode race boards at incredibly high speeds across the planet, dressed in ridiculous flouro colours. They were filmed in far off extreme locations, riding in great style surrounded by fabulous exotic mountain scenery. However, in the UK the hard boot, race board riders were often called 'Euro-faggots,' because of the image created by their counterparts in the Alps, and although some Brits had chosen to copy this style most had gone for the cooler freestyle image. I had ridden in both hards and softs, and was aware of the benefits of each discipline, and each was able to open the magic door to my floating world in their own way.

The one American that I admired most, and who was at the top of his game at this time, was Craig Kelly. He was a part of the Mount Baker Hard Core based in the north west of America, where a snowboard epicentre had developed devoid of all the hype. He had become a backcountry expert and strong competitor, and one who seemed to carry the very soul of snowboarding on his shoulders. At the pinnacle of his success in competition, he had decided to bail out of the demanding contest circuit. Understated, but great to watch on film, he just got on with snowboarding for the love of it. His change of direction spearheaded a growing anti-competition movement, which followed in the footsteps of extreme rider Tom Burt. The movement led to great videos of our heroes just snowboarding and being paid for doing it, and the films of these exploits became more and more addictive. The limits of extreme were being pushed now to new levels of crazy risk. I had no desire to watch competitions on film, but could watch free riding in perfect conditions endlessly. Craig Kelly maintained his lifestyle without competition for many years, until tragically his own life ended when he was avalanched.

We had our overseas heroes, and now we were ready for our own UK plastic heroes, although at this time we didn't even have a UK colour magazine dealing with purely snowboarding. *Skateboard* magazine had covered the Sheffield event with a small section in the magazine, as snowboarding had not quite emerged from the shadows. With my position with the guesthouse and stable job, combined with my blunt introduction to the expanding British snowboard scene, I was able to devote some energy and time to what was to become a very exciting time in the growth of the sport. Being not such a youngster though meant that I wasn't as physically flexible as the kids and was quite prepared to take a role in organising. I also tried to help guide things when they went too wayward!

If the first epic dry slope competition held in Sheffield was the catalyst to kick-start the UK scene and the following summer's offer of three competitions would really establish the future of small comps across the country. These more localised events meant that young kids, who couldn't travel far, were given the chance to become involved in the scene through a nearby contest. In addition it would enable regional centres to develop around a slope, shop or in some cases a local hero.

While I was going to Pembrey Ski Slope in 1989 to ride and teach, I kept one beady eye on an area of Swansea named Morfa. It was in this run down industrial zone that the infamous Morfa skate ramp was situated, and it was here that a good friend of mine, Roger Bateman, was optimistically building a new artificial ski slope. Roger was a well-known Swansea character who ran a successful travel agency business predominately based around skiing holidays. His 'big' annual ski trips to the Alps were legendary amongst Swansea skiers, and to enhance the ski holiday experience for his holiday clients he had even built a very small indoor plastic ski slope in 1980, just on the edge of town. Luckily, it was situated near my office, and the little shabby building was conveniently sandwiched between a brothel and a gym. Roger had kindly given me the key, so that I could stroll over at lunchtimes, and on my way over I would nod to the loitering prostitutes, with my board under my arm, and then go and ride the little slope for half an hour. Despite the slope only being long enough for three turns, what an oasis from boring work it was!

The new slope being developed at Morfa was an outdoor construction about one hundred and thirty metres long, with gentle rollers put in at regular intervals. The surface was made from Ski Tech a denser type of matting than Dendix, and this enabled it to hold the board edges very well. Strategically placed at the bottom was a large bank intended to slow you down, but which fortuitously allowed the more skilled rider to finish off a fast run with a large circular carved turn. The top of the slope ended with a long perpendicular ridge, along which the London trains sped east, and whenever one of these noisy trains rumbled past they gave the chilling impression of an impending avalanche! Luckily for me Roger, also being a surfer, was open to the idea of having snowboarding at the slope, which was in complete contrast to many other dry slopes at this time. Consequently, as long as there were no major injuries or pending lawsuits, Roger was happy.

The slope finally opened in October 1989, and the race skiers wanted to put on a big ski race for the official opening. I asked Roger whether we could organise a snowboard competition too, and he agreed so long as it was in a semblance of control! Roger being a long time surfer and aware of the skate scene nearby, knew of the potential controversy between all the different factions involved. He was, however, naturally drawn to snowboarding because of his surfing roots, and the official opening was set for June the following year, and in the meantime I taught there much more than Pembrey.

The Swansea scene expanded rapidly and a bunch of early riders eagerly wanted to learn the techniques involved in jumping and using a ramp. I began by teaching them a very basic jump on the slope, and from there moved them on to a small ramp, but plagued by litigation worries I soon had to leave them to their own devices. Roger also being concerned about the legal implications decided that a club night would be the answer for the advancement of freestyle snowboarding, at their own risk! As a result it wasn't long before we had a talented bunch of freestylers like the dread locked Simon Hennessey, Richard Stephenson, Gavin Davies and Simon Abra. Meanwhile at Pembrey slope, Neville Davies who worked there, kept the freestyle scene going with the occasional help from me, saving me a long drive over to Pembrey.

I was surprised one day when an enthusiast from Cardiff, some forty miles away, Malcolm Harvey, turned up at the slope for lessons, a guy that typified the developing American snowboard image and had been inspired by the film *Apocalypse Snow*. He had also been captivated when he witnessed someone on a snowboard in an Andorran ski resort. He had developed a passion for Indie music by bands like The Pixies, the Seattle grunge sound and hip hop derivatives. His cool casual clothing straight from the shops of the skate and surf manufacturers presented the latest image of the twentieth century snowboarder. He was keen to board well, and teaching him was not a challenge, as he could skate, surf and now snowboard.

Once he had learned the basics he was able to attempt the more difficult tricks such as getting airs, which in turn meant that he could gradually try the more crazily named freestyle tricks such as, nose bones, mute airs, roast beefs or nuclear airs! Most of these names developed from existing skateboard moves, and Malcolm became quite adept at them and liked nothing better than pulling an air off the ramp or natural terrain and holding a mid-air pose for the gawking onlookers, and then making a good landing. This type of aerial coolness became the magnetic draw for young potential snowboarders, especially those from a skating background. All you had to do was to add some headphones with good music on, and you were 'King of the World', and if someone happened to take a midair shot of you, the bedroom wall would never look the same again.

Over the years Malcolm's technique improved greatly by observing myself and other good riders, and by coming to training events with me, where he sharply observed the riders I worked with. Personally I was able to benefit from our relationship by getting his balanced witty take on this developing snowboard scene. We also benefited from the new steady stream of snowboarders he introduced from his hometown of Cardiff, and when Evo, the manager of the City Surf shop in Cardiff, started a sub-scene quickly developed there. This new scene in Cardiff brought some cool characters to Swansea for lessons and to enjoy the snowboard nights that developed there. One wild skater that came down was Matthew Pritchard, and along with Lee Dainton, White Room skater, they went on one of Evo's trips to our chalet in Les Arcs.

Evening entertainment for them was to video their usual insane acts and this led to 'Pritchard v Dainton', *'Dirty Sanchez'*; and beyond. It soon became apparent that some of the skating fraternity from around the country were realising the similarity of both sports and the two scenes began to morph into each other.

Malcolm achieved fifteenth overall on snow, and seventh overall in a dry slope series, but rather than struggling to be the best was happy enough to just enjoy the competitions. His attitude typified the spirit of the era, and was in total conflict with the financial and egoistical interests that later took over the sport. For this wave of cool laid-back boarders that began to appear around this time, the hard boots and alpine boards of central Europe were not for them and they were miles away from the accepted image of alpine skiing.

CHAPTER TWELVE — 1989 to 1991

— THE ASSOCIATION —

*'Why is loneliness such a drag, and friendship
a passing cloud of camaraderie?'*

Since the early 'formation' of the British Snowboard Association with Paul Welsh, Dave Furneau and Jeremy Sladen, there had been no real action to develop the project, until more enthusiasts were inspired to join the party. Along with the mysterious ethics of Angel Lights and an odd article written in *Skier* magazine by Paul Welsh, Jeremy became concerned and a confrontation loomed between them. At a later heated meeting held in Channel View, after the first Swansea competition, it was agreed to have elected officials! Jeremy cared about the future of snowboarding and was outspoken enough to stand up to Paul Welsh and his strange pal Dorky. The new move brought all areas of the UK together after the British Snowboard Association (BSA) was reformed and constituted at Swansea.

The first issue of *Snowboard!* magazine was published in September 1990 and announced that Eddie Spearing was now the chairman, Dave Furneau the secretary, Rob Needham the treasurer and, membership, Andy Huggins the English rep, Paul

Welsh the Scottish rep, but was quickly replaced by Scott Hanton and Grant Roberts. The revolt over, we could now promote snowboarding in our own inimitable British way. We now had a web of riders across the UK and this joining up of little areas of development brought us together like the pieces of a jigsaw, but of course the Internet was unheard of at this time and communication was only by telephone, fax and the odd letter.

The important regional areas currently developing were Swansea, Birmingham, Swadlincote, Rossendale, Sheffield, Glasgow, Norwich, Aldershot, Hillingdon and Hemel Hempstead. By general discussion amongst us it was possible to arrive at some sort of teaching method. I volunteered to write the first teaching manual and was given a draft manual from America, which was called a *Snowboard Ski Instruction Manual*, a worrying title to start with. However, when I began to read it and got lost in 'philosophy,' 'marketing-promotional programs' and 'self propelling movements' I used it to prop the door open!

I had inadvertently stumbled across the crux of the problem that the skiing fraternity were failing to grasp. Snowboarding itself had become a revolution on the slopes, and by learning from our own mistakes we were able to have a new philosophy backed up by our crazy outlook. It would have been so easy to take the skiing template and overlay it on snowboarding, but that just wasn't going to happen. And the more resorts that banned snowboarding just made the lifestyle more attractive to the rebels being drawn to it. By calling a snowboard a 'snowboard ski' it was linking it to a discipline of skiing, but in my opinion and my fellow snowboarders this was sad to the core!

I sat in front of a pile of blank paper and became amazed how blank paper can make your mind blank too. The first problem to overcome was identifying the type of people that we would be teaching and would become our future instructors. Many would come from city skating backgrounds and therefore would not be *au fait* with the world of skiing, so we needed simplicity, safety and fun first. The layers of restrictive bureaucracy could come later as it always does, as I believed that a man's style remains his own, and this would lay down boundaries but would not turn instructors into robots. Individual development and experimentation would be needed to find our own way, balanced against the boundaries of teaching a potentially dangerous sport. No psychology or proprioception required at this stage!

Amazingly, with the help of the likes of Dave Furneau, Ian Cocking Rob Needham and Martin Drayton a draft manual was completed and a beginners guide laid out for all to see, and after a few tweaks were made the new manual was ready to go. The first courses were run in Swansea and then Ackers Trust in Birmingham, thus igniting the teaching fuse and immediately several other slopes asked for our help.

Typically the sport spread from the few slopes

that had allowed development to the many new slopes, and consequently a vibrant scene would develop around the brave new slope. Going around the country to experience new places and the myriad of dry slopes in strange places was fascinating for me. For many years, I encountered really interesting and fun people training to be instructors, which made the task very enjoyable. Often I would have to change their riding styles over the weekend, which could be hard work and was mainly due to ingrained habits from another sport, usually skating or surfing! The initiation of a turn would frequently be a sticking point and this would be changed with specific exercises to iron out these quirks. Despite these challenges at the end of a weekend of hard work, the improvements in these intrepid riders would be reward enough for me. Going straight back to work on the Monday totally exhausted, however, took its toll eventually. I was struggling to balance work, snowboarding and domestic life sometimes and burning the candle at both ends, and in the middle!

Once we started to make inroads though, the system spread quickly and offshoots went in all directions. At Swadlincote, for instance, Julian Palmer had started teaching and one of his trainees was Carl Ringelberg. Once Carl was competent he looked for a slope closer to his home to ride on so tried Telford slope. They didn't allow boarding so he had to sneak on at night, until he found that Gloucester slope was amenable and started riding there alone. Carl joined our instructor courses, and this set him off on a teaching path at Gloucester, and consequently a great scene developed there over the following years.

Characters were drawn to the scene like a magnet, and so the web grew from the originals at a slope to the protégés. Chod in North Wales spawned Jonny Barr and Martin Robinson who enthusiastically got involved in many parts of the national scene, like family.

However, in the mountain resorts the conflict between skiers and snowboarders was escalating, and wasn't helped by out of control beginner snowboarders crashing into skiers! Although we knew that teaching and education were the answer to this, informal investigation showed that in many cases holiday skiers were hiring boards for half a day to 'give it a go.' Their ability to ski already excused them from having lessons and they expected to be able to ride one immediately. To their surprise everything was different and they couldn't control the board, crashing into anyone in their path. The board was grumpily returned to the hire shop and off they went happily on their skis, leaving the blame at the foot of snowboarders, when it was, in fact, the quasi-snowboard skiers!

We were now beginning to attract a cross-section of society to learn and become instructors and inner city kids that felt unwelcome in skiing circles were encouraged to progress at dry slopes, and hopefully keep out of trouble. They felt at home with our laid back attitude and had found a new direction in their everyday lives.

The BSA was also able to promote its own contests culminating in the grand final at Hemel Hempstead in 1990. That year we had increased the number of contests to three; the first at Ackers Trust in Birmingham, followed by the Swansea event, and then the 'The British Open Championships' at Hemel Hempstead. Each venue had its own quirks and design that we adapted to but the overall theme was a snowboard get-together and party.

The Swansea event was finalised with Roger the owners blessing and would coincide with the official opening of the Swansea slope. I had been promised support from my contacts at the Sheffield competition and proceeded to get a large ramp built. The keen riders and the stalwarts had confirmed that they would make the journey down to join a handful of locals. The ramp that was built was able to launch riders high and far down the slope resulting in injury if the landing was wrong, but the kudos was eagerly accepted as a part of the hardcore snowboard image. In addition the Ski Council of Wales (SCOW) agreed to put on a sponsored ski race, followed by our slalom race. Then the snowboard freestyle would take place after the Major had made the awards, followed by a big snowboard party in town.

As the day of this big event dawned I was nervous and excited. This was new ground for me, and fortunately it was a lovely sunny day and the slope looked pristine. I was there early and triple checked everything was ready, while Roger was strutting about with a grin on his face and the years of red tape and dealing with the council were forgotten about. Roger's rotund, ever cheerful father-in-law, Harold, was a bigger klazomaniac than usual and had the new arrivals either in stitches or blushing madly. The feeling of anticipation was high and the mixture of this with the bright morning sun on the sleepy slope provided a strong concoction of addictive fun. I printed t-shirts with a picture of a snowboarder doing a nose grab and his head exploding, drawn by my friend Steve, with the caption 'Snowboard your brains out!'

The cars arrived steadily and the skiers began to prepare their armoured practice runs and in stark contrast the laid back boarders who strolled in, casually dressed with boards under their arms chatting. From my viewpoint at the top of the slope I could see shiny car tops in all directions. The slope was packed with people and the buzzing amphitheatre was ready for a show.

The skin-tight skiers professionally completed their two solo timed runs with the emphasis on being worried about hundredths of seconds difference. When the casual boarders got on the slope with their 'tongue in cheek' menacing attitude for the slalom the cultural differences between the two sports was clearly evident. It appeared to look like homogenised skiing against flamboyant snowboarding, and only the far off American, Glen Plake, with his colourful Mohican hairstyle, spear-headed any sort of change in rigid ski attitudes.

Names such as Tudor Thomas (Chod) from North Wales and Darren Williamson, with his pineapple head haircut, became etched in 'glory,' especially when Mark Webster, sporting a red dressing gown managed to nut the woman Major with his peaked hat on being presented with a medal. That was probably her first and last encounter with snowboarders! Katrina Chiew was the first girl to bravely compete and went on to train with us and set up 'Snowboard Elite' a long term teaching venture.

Then the ramp was dragged out and the audience level rose to fever pitch as the flamboyant youth began to fly through the air in weird and wonderful poses, accompanied by a never ending tune of jeers and mickey taking. Team Gnats Chuff wore blood red dressing gowns and looked ethereal flying off the ramp, and the blood flowed as a supplemental prize. I was stoked to see a big crew of boarders going for it and pushing the limits for dry slopes. After the visually boring slalom it was impressive; even some of the ground tricks performed on the way to the ramps, for added fun and points. What became blatantly evident during this mayhem was that the riders were having a lot of fun regardless of the results.

In the official part of the freestyle, big airs by Mark Webster, Marc Chester and Ben Smith gave them the top places, but the 'Team Gnats Chuff' flying display off the ramp in their red dressing gowns stole the show at the end.

Now that some of the riders were sponsored by the likes of Burton, Sims, K2 and Nitro and there was an air of importance about them, but what it really meant was that they were given a free board or two! Those riders had to put some effort in at the right time, although some of the unsponsored riders were just as capable. The Scottish crew had made the long trip down the endless motorways and showed that they could go big on plastic, as well as on snow. Wounds patched up we retired to the infamous 'Cricketers Pub' for the start of a big night out, and for me the stress of organising the day had long gone. The highlight of the night was the walk to town, when Darren 'Pineapple Head' suddenly decided to free climb up a five-storey office block, in the dark! I could only visualise the headlines in the local paper the next day if it had gone wrong. Adrenalin moment over, the party resumed.

In September 1990 the summer roadshow rolled on to Hemel Hempstead for the final to crown the overall champions. If Swansea was a pretty, ugly town on a sweeping tidal bay, then Hemel was a bland, brand new town on the edge of Greater London. The main slope was slower than at Swansea, but it had the added 'bonus' of an adjoining bone-shaking mogul field, just in case you hadn't snapped your fingers on the main slope, you could gamble a bit higher by trying a rodeo ride through the bumps!

As it was another blue-sky day and the matting ran a bit slower than usual, but the summery atmosphere made up for it. The slalom ran uneventfully, and the final placing for the British Championships was settled in quite a surprisingly competitive way. Of course the sponsored riders needed some sort of result to impress their masters, but were eclipsed by our Dutch hero, Noel Gaddo, who had flown in and proceeded to win the open slalom title. However, the British title went to Chod, from Llandudno slope, where his time spent sneaking on to the slope had paid off as he had now perfected his quick turning wiggle. Unsponsored rider Lucas Dalglish, a chef working in Val d'Isere, took a deserved third place, and we had one well-padded female entrant... Anne McCluskey!

After a leisurely, boisterous lunch in the sun, the freestyle practice began in earnest and the crowd woke up. Now the fun began as riders attempted strange obstacles that were placed on the slope for skate-type tricks, and this was followed by three ramps in a row designed for a variety of big airs. The air tricks were getting better all the time, and snow boy, Alan Innes, took the overall and event champion title, with big stylish airs that even impressed the bar staff. Mark Webster took second place, and had been slowly creeping up the ladder with his eyes firmly fixed on the top spot.

However, in true snowboard fashion the best event was more fun than competitive, as an expression session took place in the mogul field.

Chod invented a new prone position for going fast over bumps, much to the amusement of everyone. But stealing the show, and the day by a mile, was the well-endowed Andrew Silver. He swiftly stripped stark naked and gingerly put a metal lift pole between his bare legs and rode the draglift to the top! Then to wincing sounds from the blokes, and laughter and gasps from the attentive girls, he rode the dendix bump field back down, narrowly avoiding circumcising himself! We laughed all the way down the M4 back to Swansea.

So this unique British scene of a plastic summer series had now given the riders a backdrop to show off their blossoming skills. The first three issues of *Snowboard* magazine, a supplement in *Skateboard* magazine, had covered the new series and the second issue had a great cover shot of Noel Gaddo in full flight, going off the Hemel ramp. He looked like a matador, except that he was dressed in gay clothing and a shiny pink helmet! This was totally acceptable for the era as multi-bright coloured clothing was in. The impact of this media coverage meant that riders needed the contests more regularly and the advertisers could increase their budgets and hopefully their sales. These complex relationships were growing, but at the same time there was a definite attitude that competition should not be taken too seriously from the majority of riders, myself included. I always felt that life was greater than our little endeavours and big egos, and in America a backlash against competition had really gained a lot of ground.

Around the world board manufacturers were feeling the popularity of snowboarding, especially Burton as they had improved their freestyle boards and the staple Burton 'Air' was becoming very popular. However, Tom Sims had licensed Vision to make Sims boards, and also approached DNR in Europe to make boards. This led to Tom Sims and Vision in a complex legal battle and Sims seemed to be in court more than on the mountain. On top of that the Sims v Burton board design affray had switched, and Burton took the lead for good. Burton boards had left their inefficient designs in the retro bin and moved on to reliable performing boards in an ever-increasing range. Many other new brands mushroomed in this period in a similar fashion to surf and skateboards, and some riders left their companies to set up their own hardcore brands. These had credibility with the youngsters and flourished with their hardcore image promoted by a hardcore rider. The shapes of boards had moved in to a new phase, and lollipop stick shapes were becoming the norm. Twin tips, which were symmetrical and had the nose and tail exactly the same shape, had been designed by Barfoot, and worked very well for freestyle. The original shapes that had evolved from surfboards had almost died out, but they still lurked somewhere in the background. Racing designs were exciting too, as the offset asymmetric race board had been developed, and the Swiss Nidecker board, the 'Concept,' rode very well. This was a flourishing period to be in, as innovation in board design was moving at a terrific pace, probably its fastest ever.

The snowboard boots that had caused us so much aggravation in the early days were now progressing to high levels. Burton, Airwalk and Okay softs were available for freestyle and general riding, and Raichle and UPS had made hard snowboard boots that flexed sideways, unlike ski boots that were too stiff for snowboarding, and needed different qualities.

In mountain clothing the surf companies had moved in swiftly, and they often produced low quality jackets and pants, but competitively priced for a surf-type generation, with the likes of O'Neill, Quiksilver and Rip Curl seeing a growing market. Bamboo Curtain, Chiemsee and Oxbow were also competing in this exciting opportunity and were stocked in a lot of shops. Ski wear became seriously unfashionable now, and boarder only companies like Wave Rave and Burton made specific, high-quality technical kit, that came with an equally high price tag. Distinct features for boarders were added like bum and knee patches as being attached to your board meant that a lot of time was spent on your backside or knees between rides. Also the designs had a looser fit than for skiing that suited the wild freestyle moves and the new image. The colours remained block and bright generally, and in the UK we had a few excellent little companies start up like Kaos, and later, Mother, Dope, Bantu, Raggy and

O'shea.

Kaos were an integral part of the British scene, and boss Ian Felton ensured that chaos drove the company. He sponsored the hardcore Scottish crew and went to a lot of events and happenings, bringing inevitable chaos with him. His company had originally developed from 'the Nutty Bollox Ski team', and had some cool casual stuff in the range. Kaos advertised heavily in the British scene and tried to be the coolest company, whilst verging on the edge of madness. A tricky balancing act, and that's without balancing the financial books!

Commercially the UK scene was set to explode with products and, therefore, needed shops to sell their wares from. A lot of the existing, ski, boat and fishing shops that sold some product didn't quite suit the image. Dave Furneau and Mon Barbour set up SS20 in Oxford in 1988, as a Skateboard and Snowboard only shop. When they approached the bank manager for a loan, he asked Dave what a snowboard was! Dave just replied that it was going to be big... music to the ears of a bank manager! Dave kept working in his other job, but the shop was just what the industry wanted. So more snowboard shops appeared like 'The Snowboard Academy,' in Aviemore, and later my own effort, 'The White Room'. The existing ski, windsurf, and skate shops joined the party too, especially when the staff and owners learnt to snowboard. Names like Grand Prix, Mach and Freedom Sports became household in the scene, and chain shops such as Ellis Brigham also became big players, in a small expanding market.

In this pre-Internet age the shops had to provide a full service for budding customers. They advised on what set up you needed for your personal ride, and this took expertise, and many a novice bought the wrong board or boots without taking advice. The shops were really useful and needed, and best staffed by snowboarders, which brought another layer of work for the existing riders.

Mike 'Peanut' Turner, 1967.

Mike 'Peanut' Turner, 1982, August Caswell on Morey Boogie.

Geoff Parr in Swansea Park using homemade board., 1985.
Photo by Kevin Jones.

Geoff Parr at First Just Ski Camp, 1989. Photo by Clive Boden.

Tudor 'Chod' Evans and Jonno Gibbins at Pembrey dry slope, 1991.

Lou Cyrrie and Kafi with a selection of Swell Panik snowboards, 1993.

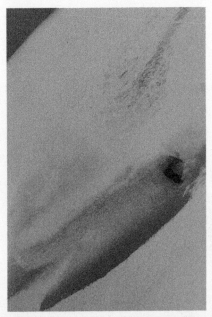

Geoff Parr, well off piste in Kaprun, Austria with photographer Sang Tang risking being caught in an avalanche, 1995.

Pete Williams surfing in Sri Lanka, 2008. Photo Lesley Parr.

— ARE YOU READY, EDDIE —

*'The nucleus is firmly established, the fuse is lit,
and the popular explosion is happening!' –
Eddie Spearing: Edition 1, SUK.*

E very once in a while I would get fed up with the sight of the diamond brush shapes of the dry slope, and having to watch the daily stolen car being burned on the hill opposite the slope by the local misguided youth. To get away from it all I would go surfing, as sitting in the ocean cleansed my mind and refreshed me, ready for more teaching.

Around that time Jonno Gibbins had come to stay and help out at Channel View, as he was getting deeper into surfing and the snowboard scene. I would advise him of the best place to surf that day, depending on tide and wind, and then I would go to work. He would go for a crowd-free surf once the work was done in the guesthouse, and I would join him on weekends and light evenings. Jonno's main aim though, was to practise his snowboarding at the slope, and he was getting very good at freestyle and slalom. We managed to do both activities together and enjoyed the camaraderie and many hours of fun.

Despite these fun sorties, the demand for lessons for beginners and instructors was growing by the week. I found myself increasingly teaching, faxing, writing letters and on the phone arranging courses. It had very swiftly become a reliably hectic pastime.

New people were coming into my life through snowboarding and the one of those was Eddie Spearing, who I met originally at the first Swansea comp. I had spotted a rider who was having problems at the bottom of the slope during the slalom and trying to fix his snapped hard binding. He had dark wavy hair and round-rimmed specs, and he was cussing and asking for tools. I went over to him and made a not too unreasonable suggestion to him, and he immediately snapped back at me that he was a qualified engineer! I laughed at this man who seemed to have the impatience of a child, but took to him straight away. Then, when he became chairman of the BSA, we worked together for many years and were frequently on the same wavelength.

He was intelligent, sharp-witted, short-tempered, headstrong, funny (when he didn't mean to be), broad-shouldered, and his part Spanish heritage came through in heated moments! However, he became the centre of the British snowboarding world, and quite rightly so in my humble opinion.

Eddie had met early pioneer, Dave Furneau, through skating and moved in with him temporarily as he was working nearby, and this led Eddie into snowboarding, and he slowly got more and more involved. When Eddie met one of Dave's skate and snowboard friends, Rob Needham, he was suddenly set off on a new path. Rob, who was sponsored by

Acid Snow, knew that the makers, Al and Gus, needed an engineer to help build their new snowboard press. So Rob made the connections, steering Eddie to firstly, take a long drive to Scotland to sample their famous parties, and secondly, design the desired press. He finally designed and assembled the press while, coincidentally, the editor from *Skateboard!* was interviewing Al and Gus about Acid Snow. His name was Steve Kane, and he took the opportunity to ask Ed to be his technical editor, and Ed jumped at the chance, and the pinball was off.

Eddie and newcomer, Stig, were thrown together because of *Skateboard!*, and were responsible for putting articles and photos about snowboarding in the mag. They extended this to some flimsy pullouts, called *Snowboard!* for three issues, but the editor, Steve Kane, was soon forced to abandon snowboarding as the owners put the business into liquidation. Steve, Eddie and photographers Stig and Duffy were left in debt and out of work, which was a sign of the times in the precarious magazine industry.

Straight away Eddie and Stig saw an opportunity and got together in a pub in Bath, and after thrashing it over, decided to go for it and produce the first proper full coloured snowboard magazine for their land. They decided to call the magazine *Snowboard UK*, or *SUK* for short. However, for all their vision, they still had to do it on a shoestring, and they didn't know what an arduous task they were about to venture into. Stig's parents provided the premises above their carpet warehouse in Kidderminster, and the two of them burned the midnight oil with their youthful energy. It was a steep learning curve, but their punk attitude to do it their own way drove them. Long days and nights working hard were finalised when Eddie would say, 'That's all it's going to get!' And another edition was produced, ready or not.

So it was by October 1991 Eddie and Stig launched *Snowboard UK*. The mag became the mouthpiece of British snowboarding and was irreverent, slightly offensive and funny. At the same time, it kept us up-to-date with the winding path that snowboarding was taking. The best riders got coverage and had the Mickey taken out of them, and local heroes were created, and we could finally see photos of Brits, instead of Americans. It rightly created controversy in doing its job, but it was a magic moment in British boarding that would be hard to recreate. It was the gel that had been missing to pull us all together, just like a genie popping out of a bottle.

By gathering all aspects of British snowboarding for the magazine Eddie was regularly in touch with riders, trade, photographers and snow-based organisations. Being the Chairman of the BSA as well conveniently placed Eddie at the heart of all of it. Although, once we started the BSA, we had to work for little or nothing, as there were no funds at all, which meant that we all needed other sources of income to keep it going. The committee were dedicated volunteers for the majority of the time and squeezed chores in where they could. Hence the magazine gave Eddie the ability to cover both jobs, on a variable meagre income, although he was never short of a snowboard or two, or the latest clothing!

SUK rock and rolled its way through the years of expansion in snowboarding, or should I say hip-hopped its way. Eddie was into hip-hop and techno, and regularly complained about 'old' music at comps. Music, freestyle images and a new wave feel helped the mag to portray a dynamic movement. This movement now offered a tangible membership of a cult club to new riders, via the magazine. This simultaneously allowed snowboarding to creep into popular culture here, as in America. Snowboarding found itself linked to the underground youth culture, which also brought a problem for the mag, as the skin-tight racing, hard boot scene didn't fit this image neatly. Freestyle dominated the British scene, but it was different in the rest of Europe, so it was a fine line that Eddie and Stig walked, and they did it well to maintain their credibility. They didn't ignore the hard booters, but gave the majority of the space to freestyle and freeriding. Snowboard 'skiers' in disguise were circumnavigated, and probably grumbled into their hard boots.

Another conflict of interest was the fact that Eddie was chairman of the BSA, so to help the BSA he put a page in the mag with all the latest official news, but in rest of the mag he and Stig did what they wanted! This solved a media issue for the BSA and saved on hundreds of stamps, letters and envelopes. It also showed that the magazine was not BSA influenced in its reporting of the British scene.

It would be fair to say that what Eddie and Stig achieved with this colourful magazine was immense. It increased the number of boarders annually at a great rate, and it armed them with protocol, board information and culture. It was the centre of the swirling vortex that was a fast moving lifestyle busting down doors, and if you were cool you could get your picture in a national mag!

CHAPTER FOURTEEN — 1988 to 1991

— A VERY BRITISH
SNOWBOARD CHAMPIONSHIP —

'Spin, Flip, Grab 'n Glide — Starbound!'

In Scotland, in March 1988, the hardcore Aberdeen crew had organised the first British snow championships at Glenshee, and there were nine entrants. In 1989 they did the same again, and there were twenty-five entrants.

Despite these seemingly straightforward facts, that first British snow championships at Glenshee really only happened by chance. It was due to Adrian Corrigal, who was brought up in Aberdeen, and hung out with his schoolmates at the Ramp Warehouse, where they were into BMX and skating.

In 1985 two of his schoolmates, Stuart Duncan and Cammy Bain, bought Burton Elite 150's and moon boots, and they all tried riding at Glenshee and on the local golf course. They immediately loved the buzz from using the natural terrain and the speed rush, but they hated the Glenshee lifts, and considered skiing a rich person's sport. Fellow schoolmates, Mark Webster and Steve Crampton, joined them in their exploits and they all persevered at snowboarding, eventually progressing to become a vital part of the British scene.

They would spend winter weekends looking for useable snow in isolation from any other boarders, but early on they had one shock when they saw a strange snowboarder arrive at the Glenshee car park. He had a new Burton Safari board with matching Burton clothes, and to them looked almost God-like. They were stunned to find out that it was Huw Parsons from Outdoor Action in Cardiff. They had never seen equipment like it and neither had they seen such an advanced rider. It was because of this chance meeting that Adrian got his first Barfoot snowboard from Huw and never looked back. Their isolated snowboard world had been irrevocably changed forever by Huw's appearance.

A year or so later, Adrian happened to be in Glasgow and noticed that the Scottish Ski Show was on. So he wandered in and found the Sun stand, and then cheekily asked if they could have a snowboard championship at their Sun Week in Glenshee. Expecting a polite refusal, he was surprised to find that they were happy to allocate one day to it, and Adrian even cajoled them into putting up some prize money. They casually named it the first British Snowboard Championships.

Noel Gaddo, Stuart Duncan, Cammy Bain and Adrian Corrigal optimistically put the day together, and they competed along with Huw Parsons, Dave Furneau, Ian Cocking, Rob Needham and Mark Tucker, all from the south. They used the existing framework of the Glenshee Snow Fun Week, which had a different snow activity for each day of the week. Pernod was the main sponsor of the fun week and used the appropriate caption 'Free The Spirit.' Burton Snowboards, 7th Wave and Ski-Surf Ecosse weighed in early to sponsor this inaugural snowboard slalom race. It must have been a strange feeling for the nine pioneers to be holding the competition, and set the scene for many more championships to come. A classic photo taken of them all in a group is, to my mind, one of the iconic British snowboard shots.

As it happened the snow conditions were as variable as the weather, but they managed to hold the timed slalom course and Huw Parsons easily won it. Then this was followed by an impromptu freestyle event using some quickly dug snow banks for hits, Dave Furneau won that. Nevertheless, the official cup was for the slalom only, so Huw Parsons became the first ever British snowboard champion. Most of the entrants were on early Burton boards and a few on original Sims boards, but Huw wisely rode a Burton Safari to race on, and the Sims Ultimate to compete in the freestyle. This neatly demonstrated the two main directions that board development was proceeding in during those early days. Also the party afterwards demonstrated the differing directions that the hardcore Scottish crew and Huw were going in. Huw was a serious mountain man and not a drinker, so the American-style snowboard rock star image was not for him.

The Scottish crew were confirmed party animals, but despite this it was still the first gathering of snowboarders from across the British Isles for a national event.

With the BSA revamped, the 1990 snow championships were 'slightly' more organised and held in the newly opened Aonach Mor, on Ben Nevis. This curious resort encompassed a more suitable set up for accommodation and was able to deal with the increasing numbers of entrants. Running this event became a good learning curve for the BSA in competition management on the mountain, but we were understandably treated with suspicion and kept at a good arms length by the Nevis Range management.

We were not given a prime spot with easy lift access. Instead they put out us on the 'Headwall.' This is particularly a problem if you have to carry all the equipment and, although the competitors didn't mind, I found out how difficult it can be on the mountain compared to a dry slope. The weather was that classic Scottish mix... yin and yang, or four seasons in one day!

Some standout happenings for me were seeing Ptarmigan fly by, a bust up in the hotel with Angel Lights, and experiencing a dreary ceilidh. A ceilidh in Gaelic means a gathering, but the music for a bunch of rebel snowboarders was completely misplaced. A lot of the boarders managed to book into rustic wooden cabins, while I had to book in to a guesthouse in Fort William and slept in the attic accessed by a ladder! Jeremy and his crew had a wild party in their log cabin, which resulted in a lot of damage. The next day they felt bad about it and went to B&Q for materials, and fixed the cabin back up – Rebels with a B&Q card!

This event at Aonach Mor had attracted some fifty boarders to enter, so to accommodate the growing interest in snowboarding the following year we moved the competition to the recognised top resort in Scotland, Aviemore. The event was planned for March and was going to be the first real big snowboard event on British snow. There were about ninety competitors to deal with, along with a lot of industry involvement, and plenty of commercial wheeling and dealing.

The seriously monotonous and long trip from South Wales to Aviemore was undertaken, with the Pembrey Dry slope boys and Malcolm from Cardiff driving their purple VW van for sixteen hours without any heating! They were more frozen than the icy mountain when they arrived, and we had to stay in flimsy caravans in the Speyside Park, so we quickly put all the gas appliances on to warm the place up. The harsh winter weather meant a bit of everything, but not a lot of warmth.

There was no doubt, however, that the warm heart of Aviemore centred around one Tony Brown. Unusually, Tony had been brought up here after a short time in London, which meant that a mixed-race lad with a cockney accent was a true local. Growing up there led him to join the army, and he became proficient at cross-country skiing, but didn't get on with recreational skiing, or the pretentious local skiers. On leaving the army, he decided to go to the Alps to improve his skiing, partly to shut some of the locals up, but once there unexpectedly saw three snowboarders cruising the pistes. He liked the look of what he saw and scammed a go. From then one he was hooked. The next time he went to the Aviemore resort, to the amazement of the locals, he was riding on a snowboard. He took great delight in sticking two fingers up to them about this. He was the first local snowboarder in Aviemore, and encountered resentment, jealousy and secret admiration.

Later, after meeting Jeremy on a Just Ski snowboard camp, he was encouraged to import a brand of boards and took on Kemper boards from the States. This led to him starting a shop in Aviemore, which he called 'The Snowboard Academy.' Over the years his lack of business experience got him into debt, and a ski chain of shops bailed him out. He was then asked to set up their new chain using his shop name and ended up in control of fourteen shops, which was exactly what he didn't want! That chain went on to become 'The Snowboard Asylum' or 'TSA' and became a major player in the UK retail scene. Tony gratefully got out, and went on to write ten *World Snowboard* guides instead.

At this third event, and as Tony was the main man in Aviemore, he warmly welcomed all the arriving snowboarders to the pub to thaw out. Impromptu parties broke out across Aviemore, and this was the biggest British snowboard party on record, and the locals could not ignore this weekend.. To document it we had photographers Sang Tan, Duffy and Stig on hand, and Scottish TV also wanted a bit of the action. The first night was a good fun warm up for the weekend's craziness.

The opening encounter was a chance to catch up with old friends, meet new ones and check out the latest hot gossip on the grapevine. Some riders had arrived early and already been up on the mountain, and consequently had interesting stories for the pub. Old friend Phil Young, from our epic bus trip across France, was there with Darren Robinson from the London skateboard shop Faze 7, run by big character 'Maltese Joe'. Joe and Darren were importing Hot and Barfoot boards, and Darren was getting back to snowboarding after his early crazy homemade board escapades. Their first encounter on the Scottish mountain was with a massive queue at the Aviemore draglift, so Darren shouted out that they were in the competition and had to get to the top fast. He jumped on the draglift, in front of a stern Scottish crowd, forgetting that he hadn't used one before! From cool boarder, he was quickly transformed into an inverted skidding tortoise being dragged up the mountain on his back, refusing to release the drag pole. It was this wonderful 'new kids on the block' attitude that had us roaring with laughter in the pub later on.

When we finally slipped and skidded our way back to our caravan after that first party night, we heard loudish music coming from our neighbours' caravan. As we didn't have any music in ours I knocked the door to ask them to turn it up, and some very old Scottish characters opened the door to their poorly lit world and thought that I was complaining. They were sat around drinking cheap whiskey, and once they understood my Sassenach accent they dragged me in, and gave me their golden liquor, and I finally got out an hour later. When I saw them next, the following evening, they had just got up and were older, pale and walked stiffly. They were clearly drinking their way out of life, as this was now their daily routine.

On the Saturday morning of the competition a blizzard arrived and helpers disappeared as quickly as the snowflakes. It came down to myself, Noel Gaddo and a couple of willing boarders, to set up the Giant Slalom course on an area allocated to us with no lift again! We carried the gates and timing gear in dribs and drabs up the mountain in a white out. A hangover from hell didn't help; I made a mental note not to drink any more whisky, ever! Any watching boarders had quickly retired to the café, but in the middle of the whiteness Noel's spirit came alive. In our white womb, he laughed a lot and we got on with the job. He said we could set the course a bit tighter so the riders could see two gates ahead in the atrociously changing visibility. The powder lay over a foot deep under our feet and if you stood still it drifted around your legs and started to bury them.

The thick blizzard created a cocoon around us. Dressed in layers and layers of clothing, with only a nose poking out from tinted goggles, it felt like I was in another swirling, snowy, white world. Deep within myself I viewed this strange scene, slightly detached and we worked and moved like stilted spacemen.

Noel finally shouted to me, 'You ride down fast, making good turns and keep them tight!'

No second telling was needed. Once the muscles responded to a new activity I rode through the blizzard, making sweet turns in the powder. Now I felt better, that floating feeling came back, and now all the cosy competitors would have to follow my line! Once I reached the finish line I walked all the way back up, close to having a heart attack. We quickly drilled the snow base to put gates inside my turns before the wind made the tracks disappear under new smooth snow. An hour later we had the course and timing all set up and the race could start.

Competitors were dragged out of the comfy cafés and sent down the barely visible course. We knew that some could have cheated, as we couldn't cover every gate, and someone had even left a bottle of booze on one of the gates buried in the snow, just for light refreshment on the way down! This was not how I had envisaged it happening, but hey we were in Britain for heaven's sake! And guess who won?

First was Danny Meier from New Zealand, second was hero of the day Noel Gaddo, the flying

Dutchman, third was Brit Ian Trotter, fourth was Dutchman Chris van den Brink and fifth Brit Lloyd Rogers. So the foreigners did well, and the first two Brits were based in the Alps, but this was racing and we were more into freestyle, of course.

The women's racing had finally come of age too, and was well fought over by seven women, with Joanna Neil first, then Lisa Fletcher and Gillian Hall third.

As usual there were grumbles from some freestylers that racing was taking precedent, and that the half pipe wasn't built ready, but due to the weather we had to put off that day's slalom until the next morning. Snowboarding needed the racing for the trade and media, and the speed freaks. Giant slalom was more natural to me as the turns were wider, but a balance had to be struck, and the more ski-type slalom would have its day. We decided that we would only call off the slalom if it wasn't ready to be run by ten o'clock the next morning, in order to start building the half pipe.

I did feel that the resort management were being unhelpful, and if this event had been held abroad there would be a better chance of good snow, weather and assistance. They certainly hadn't taken snowboarding to their hearts, and were probably sitting on the fence waiting to see how big it became. I couldn't help noticing the cold eyes of some mountain locals, steely grey with pale hard faces! A product of their environment I wondered? I didn't get the feeling we were welcome here by some, maybe it was just me but I felt like it was more like Aviemordor!

That night was a big night with a good band called 'The Buzzing Chairs,' and it was now the turn of the Brits to excel in partying, rather than on the slope. The foreigners didn't have a chance against the home-grown party animals, but I was finished by the day's activities and planned on retiring earlyish. However, Mr Kaos turned up late with sponsored bibs only to say that they were not numbered! As Kaos was paying good sponsorship money I had to rope the boys in our caravan in, as soon as they got back, and we spent the early hours writing numbers in felt pen on bibs! A very good way to sober up, but Aviemore partied on through the night.

The solemn slalom happened in the morning under calm clear weather – a miracle after the previous day, and all went to plan except that the foreigners thrashed us again. The big surprise was that North Walian, Chod, won out of the Brits, even with a poor start number, and from the women's riders Joanna Neil did the double and won the slalom in style.

Then it was all hands on building the halfpipe, which was not so bad looking across the lovely views over the Cairngorms National Park, with the beautiful Scots Pine trees giving it a distinct feel. The shiny lakes, nestled amongst woodlands and mountains gave the scene some sparkle. I noticed two lone raptors wheeling around in their own bit of sky, and I wondered how on earth they had survived the atrocious day before? However, they had made it and were relishing the mild thermals and spectacular views over their potential lunch. This was such a startling change from the blizzard whiteouts that drove into the dark recesses of anything.

During the week, the resort had half allocated a Kiwi driver and piste basher to try and push enough snow in place for a halfpipe. Simon Smith, a great young rider, directed the driver, and over several nights managed to get some snow roughly in place. Blizzards and the management hampered the exercise though, so only an icy affair was finally put together. This meant that it was a case of hand sculpting the icy walls, and it took many hands and shovels to complete our imitation white waves. The hand dug half pipe ended up about two hundred and fifty feet long and thirty feet wide, which was pretty epic for us at that time, but would be described as pretty barbaric nowadays!

The tools were abandoned as a practice session kicked off, and it rapidly became an adrenalin-fuelled session as each good rider pushed their personal limits in order to impress everyone else. The higher up they went the better, and as the first issue of *SUK* reported – 'Massive Rusty Russel was in orbit. Frontside Floaters, seven to eight feet out and forty feet long, no joking. He only managed to get three hits out of the two hundred and fifty feet pipe per run.'

Young Simon Smith had excelled at getting the half pipe finished and then performed well riding in it with the difficult McTwist flips, high above the pipe. Yet again, the excellent Alan Innes went high and smooth, and the warm up was the highlight of the weekend, and was actually better than the contest. It also gave the judges the chance to watch and home in on the new moves the riders were doing. Judging in any sport is always subjective and open to errors or favouritism, that's human nature, and snowboarding is no different. I had watched some abysmal decisions made in world surfing competitions, so to try and avoid this we coordinated and set benchmarks. We were marking against height, difficulty of trick and smoothness, but the balancing of these aspects is where the problem lies, and some of the competitors lived in a room full of mirrors.

Watching Rusty going massive certainly made me feel amazed, like watching a big wave surfer, but technical tricks done much lower didn't give me that jaw-dropping feeling. Inverted spins were clearly difficult and potentially dangerous, and warranted good marks. The judges were on a hiding to nothing, though, as some competitors thought they were the best, regardless of their performance. That's why I preferred the free sessions, where the riders can be expressive without any constraints; it takes the pressure and invisible boundaries away, and is great to watch.

The trade and egos, however, need a winner, so by the time that we ran the contest quite a few of the riders had already burned themselves out in the practice. That's the irony of these contests; did the best win? And actually, who really cares? Survival of the fittest and all that jazz, I suppose.

The showdown came to Alan Innes, last year's winner, and Mark Webster. The scores were totted up and Alan won by a whisker, and Scottish TV wanted to interview the winner. Then, after a forced recount, it was revealed that a mistake had been made, and they were joint winners! The announcement was made in the bar afterwards, and caused quite a raucous atmosphere! Alan and Mark shared the title! A fairy tale ending, probably not, but amateurs we were, and worse things have happened at a professional level.

The judges had the usual complaints, there were rider arguments about how and where you grabbed your board in the air, if at all, which was all a bit yawnish for me! And after a very long weekend no one said thanks! I wondered whether snowboarding had moved into a new phase of selfishness, as there was now an expectation that everything would be provided 'perfectly' for little cost. The activity of hiking a hill and riding down was in the distant past, and we had established a real 'sport'. I could not help thinking of it as a lifestyle or pastime, with cultural influence, but here we were on a new stepping-stone to the future, good, bad or whatever.

Being a Sunday most people quickly packed up and left to travel south, to homes and jobs. However, they left exhausted and happy having experienced a unique event in the history of British snowboarding.

The expectation was that there would be more of the same each year, especially the après bonding. The competitions would stretch way into the future, nestled around Aviemore, but for my part I was tired of the unhelpful resort management, inconsistent weather and small size of the mountains that didn't provide sheltered areas in blizzards. As I drove the long road home reflecting on the experience, I decided not to work there next year. I was burned out, and I would have a break from our snow championships, as there was enough going on in my life. Ha, ha! Blackie was laughing at me again, or else a higher force was going to flip my pinball again!

— CRYING ON THE PISTE —

'You carve, you carve, you carve!'
Jean Nerva – RIP

The Manchester dry slope scene developed around Rossendale slope and one Paul Morgan, wheeler-dealer and cool character. Paul had worked for Crystal as a ski instructor, and was based in Kaprun, Austria. While there he tried snowboarding and became hooked on it, and alternated between Austria and Rossendale for the summer seasons. On his second winter season in Kaprun, Paul had brought a friend out with him, Andrew Hindly. Andrew trod a well-worn seasonal path by proceeding to spend all his savings on partying hard. In the nick of time he got a chalet job with Crystal too, and in his chalet he was one of two staff that shopped, cooked and cleaned while going boarding, partying and getting a bit of sleep. Their chalet goulash was a great weekly treat, which the punters loved, until one day they were shopping in the supermarket.

Another chalet girl glanced in his trolley and said to them, 'I didn't know you had a dog?'

'No we haven't, Why?' replied Andrew.

'Well that frozen Fleishhound in your trolley is

dog food!' she exclaimed.

Andrew, not being able to speak German, had no idea that they had been putting dog food in their wonderful goulash. And every year the green seasonal staff go through this fun and frivolity.

On their time off Paul and Andrew boarded around Kaprun and met up with Thomas Killan, an Austrian instructor based in Kaprun. Thomas worked with the national snowboard association of Austria, called VOSS.

Once Paul was friendly with Thomas he saw a good opportunity and put forward the idea that we in the UK could train in the VOSS system, as it was world recognised for quality. Paul liaised with Thomas, and then arranged a link between the UK and Austria for snowboard instruction courses. Martin Drayton was keen to develop the snow teaching system for the UK, and I would support him. With this in mind, we both decided to go and train on one of their courses in November 1991, as this would give me valuable knowledge of their snow teaching techniques, which I could try and adapt to the dry slopes. It was going to be expensive for me, but hopefully would improve my riding at the same time. I felt that I could justify it by tying in a week's holiday in northern Italy afterwards, and the family could potter about on the glacier during the training.

This snow course was mainly for Austrians, but a smaller one had been added on for any English speakers, so we had Dutch and British on the

English-speaking course. Paul came along to do it, as he was planning to teach in Austria with Thomas. We had three Brits signed on, and Thomas took the course, as his English was excellent, but not perfect. Paul's sidekick, Andrew, had skived off chalet duties and taken an earlier course, and passed. He, however, got caught by the management and was in big trouble, probably a karmic action for the 'dog meat goulash!'

November in the mountains is often dark, due to the short days and frequent black clouds.

I drove with the family to a sullen lost valley in the Tyrolean Austrian Alps for the course. Coincidentally, I had recently read that it was also in this area where the body of 'Otzi Man' appeared out of the glacier, after 5,200 years entombed in it! It was a daunting start to what was apparently going to be a demanding course. We stayed in a beautiful wooden farmhouse with clean comfortable rooms, where pretty cows were moved in and out of the barns, and chickens ran around. It had a rustic and timeless feel, but was moodily wintry being wedged in a thin flat valley between steep claustrophobic mountains.

Over one hundred nervous boarders met for registration and our first talk, and they all brought an array of boards, old, new, racing and freestyle; the clothing was as diverse, and I didn't have any really warm pants, so wore my wife's pale green ski suit, hidden by a super thick Oxbow jumper over the top half. Great in below minus 10c temperatures in almost constant shade on a frozen glacier.

We were put through some riding exercises to sift out the varying standards of riders. We had to come down a rough bit of steep off-piste terrain making wide radius turns. Then we had to suddenly switch to smaller radius turns, and from this we were marked and put into our training groups, and then the hard work started.

We were shown how to carve the board by applying a lot of pressure through our feet into it, while at the same time we also had to lean right over until our faces were almost touching the snow. We spent the first period working on the many aspects of a carved turn that involved most parts of your body, but particularly your brain! After a few hours we started doing the beginners first exercises, but when you had to wait for your turn the cold would reach deep into your bones. My feet would sporadically freeze and thaw, and Thomas trained us like we were in the army. If he saw us shivering he would make us jump around, then if we got his instructions wrong, he would make us do press-ups on the piste. Somewhat embarrassing in front of the class and the odd tourist!

If anybody didn't finish their turns properly, then Thomas would scream at us across the piste, 'No vishy-vashy turns!' Then he would wag his finger at us, so 'vishy-vashy' became our catch phrase that week.

It was such a relief to complete that first hard physical day, but then we had to meet up an hour later for lectures. A quick tea and shower, and we went straight onto the theory of all sorts. Thomas said to us that it was going to be very tough, and that he would cry on the piste. I felt sorry for him and sympathetic, as he didn't need to do that. We spent three hours being lectured on everything and anything to do with mountains and boarding, and it was very comprehensive. I got back to the farmhouse and checked that the family had enjoyed their day, and then collapsed in bed.

And so it went on, each day felt as long as a week, and I was steadfastly burning up my internal energy reserves. Lunch had to be a quick meet up with the family to stuff some carbs down me, then straight back on the slope feeling bloated for half an hour while riding and digesting food. I was treated to press-ups on the slope a few times due to lazy errors, and there was a simmering anger building up in me that I think Thomas knew about, and may have even been manipulating on purpose. The evenings got tougher and tougher being so tired, and this felt like advanced army training now to me.

Although I was riding in hard boots and a racy-type board, I could not get the carved turns exactly as he wanted them. It took a lot of faith in your equipment to lean right over on hard ice, and press through your legs with all your might in a controlled but subtle way. On one poor run, he screamed across the piste at me that I was a wimp! It clicked… he didn't mean he was going to 'cry' on the piste. He meant that he was going to 'shout' on the piste! And shout he did, there were no tears from him, just more press-ups!

It was around the latter part of the course and I was absolutely exhausted. I went back to the farmhouse and absent-mindedly stood in the shower. I was raging with anger and I'd had enough of this course, so I was ready to quit the next morning and go and ride off-piste and laugh at the others. I could just cruise around and have a beer, and watch with the family instead. I was thoroughly pissed off, and didn't want any more of this.

I wearily decided to give it one more go the next morning, as hunger was my driver and famine my failure, but any more press-ups and I was off. I met up with the group, barely hiding my simmering anger, and started the training again. I rode like a raging bull just to annoy Thomas and to let off some of the internal steam. Then he singled me out and shouted, 'Well done, amazing you've got it!'

The anger dispersed in a flash. I smiled for the first time in ages, but I was in disbelief. I kept at it though, and finally something clicked, I was truly carving like a bird, and it was a great feeling. This had been the hard part for me all along, as I had done so much beginners work on dry slopes I didn't struggle with that, but carving hard icy pistes and rough off-piste was way more difficult. The subtlety of the movement throughout a turn, on a board balanced on a knife-edge, was incredibly difficult to master. Then, having your arms in the right place and shifting your weight correctly, as well as the dynamic power through the legs. There was a lot going on in these powerful turns internally, but it made them appear graceful and effortless from the outside.

A corner had been turned and my anger had strangely helped, and I had learned a fantastic lesson from Thomas, and hopefully all those that got angry with me over the following years understood too! Not much is for free, and there's a latent cost to learning as well.

Martin, Paul and Andrew went through their own learning curves and mental battles with Thomas 'crying' at you. Martin's feet froze more often than mine, and he needed to defrost in the café regularly just to make sure that he still had ten toes left at the end of the course! The pressure built up all week with a final day of testing, where it was expected that you would perform all the basic manoeuvres perfectly. You would also have to carve wide, medium and narrow turns down rough terrain, but would be allowed to touch the snow once with your hand. The same had to be down on piste, but you were not allowed to touch the snow with your hand at all. Then to top it off there were the written exams the night before!

There was a clear tension building amongst the Austrians, and the same with us, and laughter was rare now. We could see that quite a few Austrians were well below the standard required in riding techniques, so we didn't feel like inadequate foreigners. Martin's slalom days spent skateboarding and snowboarding gave him a great foundation, as he was able to do quick clean turns, and he copied the arm movements of in vogue Euro riders, Jean Nerva and Peter Bauer, and that impressed Thomas. He was looking more stylish on piste than many Austrians and myself.

The evening before the last day, I walked through the Austrian room for the dreaded written tests, and the atmosphere was very tense. I had overheated and had taken off my heavy Oxbow jumper, and as I walked through their test room in the wife's green ski suit, the Austrians started wolf whistling, and taking the piss out off me! Red-faced and even hotter, I quickly dashed into the safety of our room, but at least I had broken the uptight vibe for them.

Once the written tests were done, I went back and collapsed again in the farmhouse, but sleep was filled with fitful dreams of failing the practicals. The next day was sunny and very cold, while the weak sun hardly got over the steep mountainsides. Breakfast was a silent affair for me and I dragged my worn-out body to meet everyone up on the slope, in one large group. We would all be able to watch how each other got on in the practicals, which added additional pressure by having to perform in front of a big crowd. You could cut the atmosphere with a Swiss army knife!

The beginner's exercises went expectedly well for all of the English speakers, but we could, however, see some failures in the Austrian speakers already.

The off-piste carving was difficult due to the chopped up snow conditions, but it was something that I love doing, and our trainee bunch all sailed through that. Then came the greatest test, which was the smooth, precise piste carving, during which you had to leave thin perfect curved tracks on the piste and crank the board right over in the turns.

Martin went first and performed the various turns excellently, with a stylish flourish that impressed many of the watching Austrians. Then I took off and went for it, allowing a lot of speed to build up before I initiated the first turn, and then I applied massive pressure into the board. As I came out of the first turn, the spring of the board sent me flying onto the other edge, and the resulting g-force was exhilarating as the piste whizzed past my face. It was that floating feeling again! I was like a pendulum going from one edge to the other, and I briefly forgot about the test and just carved my way down, loving it. Then one edge slipped out off the snow, just for an instant, so I was forced to just touch the snow lightly with my glove! I carried on altering the size of the turns and pulled up by Thomas, I felt happy and deflated, as I may well have failed after all that. He looked at me silently and sternly, and then winked, he pointed to the others and I went over to wait with them.

Once everyone had been fully tested we went back to the training rooms where they announced our results to loud cheers for whoever had passed. Martin got best marks for the Brits; I had passed to my delight. There were wild celebrations and dejected worn out boarders spread around, which made for a strange mood in this strangest of places. Most people rushed away from that shady glacier and it left an empty feeling around the slope.

Paul went back to the UK to pursue his dream to start a snowboard teaching school with Andrew, Thomas and his girlfriend, Laura. They had come up with the name 'Boardmania,' and marketed quality snowboard teaching in Kaprun. They had a colourful image and projected serious fun on an exciting wave of a new sport, and Paul linked the Rossendale dry slope to their Austrian venture.

Despite the sudden departure of the course entrants, I was going to stay another day or so before going to Italy for a break. I also had a bottle of Peach Schnapps waiting for me that I had been eyeing all week long, in order to celebrate the end of the course.

The next morning we could ride around the fairly empty glacier as a family, but after a couple of hours I lost sight of them down one of the runs. I saw my daughter go past on the next piste, so I shot across a linking piste we had been using all week. What I didn't see though, was a thin dark rope cutting it off. Some slope staff had started putting up, but had left without putting any warnings on it. At speed I went straight through the rope and a wooden stake drilled into the ice snapped in half as I ploughed through the connecting rope. My knee, that had held together all week, twisted violently, and the old pain returned with a vengeance. I lay on the ground in agony with my old friend, the throbbing, swollen knee.

Then, to make matters worse, three Germanic skiers pulled up by skidding their skis sideways on the icy piste. The leader looked at me with contempt and said slowly and robotically, 'Snowboard... Fun... Ya!'

They laughed and sped off before I could react, so I was left to hobble to the restaurant and curse, but luckily it hadn't happened mid-training course though, as I would have failed. I sat in thankful pain and knew from experience that I had a few months to work on it before riding hard again. I gently placed my emergency supermarket plastic bag, filled with snow, on to the enlarged knee and winced. At least I had learned something from the course theory, but the piste worker had ignored the health and safety of the slopes, and was probably enjoying his traditional lunchtime beer.

The rest of the schnapps tasted even better as a painkiller that night, and the thought of a leisurely, stress-free farmhouse breakfast was paradise. An incredible journey with Thomas was over, and now European snowboarders were teaching each other, it was cool, and now I was a qualified Austrian Snowboard instructor; even crazier! A day later and we were driving away, squeezed into the narrow valleys by the big mountains, and I couldn't stop thinking about 'Otzi Man' between painful clutch changes.

This had been his area in 3,300 BC, a very long

time ago, and it was in 1991 that two tourists discovered him still half-frozen in the summer thaw. They initially thought that he was a recently deceased mountaineer, but once he was uncovered, this man had a woven grass cloak, a coat, belt, leggings, loincloth and shoes. The shoes were made of various leathers and were wide for snow use. They even had soft grass liners, way before we got snowboard boot liners!

He was carrying an axe made from Yew and Copper, a knife, a quiver with fourteen arrows, a longbow, fire-lighting stuff and spare food. He probably did smelting and high altitude shepherding.

How he ended up frozen in the glacier was even more surprising, as he had been shot in the back with an arrow. From blood analysis it appeared that he had killed two people, both with the same arrow out of his quiver, and carried a different wounded person on his back. He may have had a fatal blow to the head as well. I wondered what on earth had happened all those years ago in this valley. He has left us with a glimpse of very early life, but what about the bits in between, as just one snap shot was fascinating enough, but what had these dark valleys seen over thousands of years?

Amazingly, he had about fifty tattoos on his body that had been made with soot. These linear tattoos may not have been trendy cool ones, but probably a very early form of acupuncture, to relieve pain. I wondered how this man had spent his forty-five years in the mountains. These same powder slopes must have been a challenge, and a danger for him. While there we were, over five thousand years later, riding down those slopes for fun, but I could certainly sense his presence, and his pain.

Even in death and defrosting, modern humans argued about him, as the Italians claimed the body as theirs, because it turned out he was found just inside their legal border. The two tourists that discovered him had to go to court over discovery payments, and then other people also claimed to have found him. The husband of the couple that discovered him died before any payment was made anyway, so even thousands of years later instead of being sandwiched between the mountains and uncivilisation, he was stuck between international politics and legalities!

However, I couldn't help wondering what sort of emotions he experienced in those far away times. Just being alone high up on a white mountain, with blue skies, may have made his spirit soar above the pettiness of the other humans below. Hopefully he experienced the wonderful feelings that the mountains can sometimes provide you with. If he had known that we would be studying him, and what he had eaten, and the state of his health before he died, so many years later, what would he have thought? His violent death turned out to be our gain, only he had to spend about over five thousand years in the glacier, oblivious as the planet's history unfolded around him, but now Otzi was back amongst company again, for better or worse.

Strangely, the melancholy of this event and the area, reminded me of driving through Glencoe on a dark dismal day. I felt something deep and gloomy in both places that I found difficult to put into words, except that sombre deeds seem to leave an arcane stain that lingers on in the environment. Bad karma again? Maybe, but once out of the mountains into bustling, food crazy Italy the mood lifted. Maybe I was suffering with post course blues, recurring wounded-knee agony or even severe fatigue!

— THE WHITE ROOM —

*'Kickflip king, captive spin, masterful
motion, product potion.'*

A s if working from nine till five in an office to pay
the bills, along with teaching, running
instructor courses and organising competitions,
wasn't enough, then fate, or Blackie, landed me with
another problem. The importers of Burton
snowboards in the UK were becoming sensitive to
supplying me with new snowboards. Naturally, the
beginners that I taught wanted advice on what
equipment would be best for their future use, and
once I had assessed what would best to suit their
needs, I would order the equipment for them from
my long list of importers. As there were no shops
supplying boards in the area, it was easier for them
if I organised it, and I could also deal with any after
sales problems that arose.

Now that the industry was expanding, and shop
wars were starting to happen, a more professional
approach was required by the importers. The Burton
rep, Jonathan Weekes, rang me and said that I would
have to open a shop, or I would not be able to order
boards any more. This was fair enough, but it was
never an intention of mine to ever have a shop, and

the only option was to let a non-specialist shop pick up the trade somewhere nearby, but without having any snowboard credibility or expertise.

After much deliberation and discussion at home, I decided to make some enquiries about running a shop as it was totally alien to me. A good friend of mine, Clive, had an office service centre, taking calls for busy contractors, and he had a hardware shop attached to it. So I called in to see Clive as he rarely saw life's problems the way that others did, and as a sort of John Cleese-type character he failed to see the fine minutiae in life. In fact, he had a habit of solving your issues in one steam-rollering minute! True to form I had only called in to chat about my problem, and in a jiffy he managed to rent me one wall of the hardware shop. He showed me how to set up the business and said he would deal with any sales in the week, and I could go in on Saturdays, or when I knew someone was going to call. I walked away stunned, could it be that easy?

Now for a name! Hardly any shops had been named purely for snowboarding in the UK. The Snowboard Academy had started in Aviemore around 1990, under the 'guidance' of funny man Tony Brown, and survived through many changes. I wanted to avoid the cliché names based on snow, which was difficult, so spent a while thinking about it. A few days after my chat with Clive, I took a chance surf at Langland Bay, as this was the closest surf beach to Swansea and was easier to get to in busy times. Its sweeping bay, backed by grand homes built into the steep woods and rocky outcrops, conserved a lovely curve of green and white beach huts. The huts seemed to nestle into a hollow shoulder of the Gower, and the bay was a mix of rocky reefs and sandy areas, which at low tide could produce some classy waves on the various reefs, and obviously attracted a lot of locals. There was a local surfer saying that you should never have your funeral at low tide… as no one would turn up! If Caswell Bay was akin to a cathedral, then nearby Langland Bay was more like an amphitheatre for surf gladiators, where you could learn the art of the gingerly take-off over rocks.

I was late getting there as the tide was pushing up fast, making the reefs disappear under the murky sea, but the power of the swell kept the waves pumping. I usually sat off the peak and let the hot locals go first, and would then pick off a lesser wave, but this day the swell was big and a bit out of control and breaking anywhere. The wind had switched around to the offshore northerly direction, coming from the long curve of green and white beach huts, and the hidden tennis courts. This wind made for lovely hollow waves and the take off was just above the weedy rocky reefs but then the rest of the ride went over a softer sandy bottom so I pushed it a bit more than normal.

One fabulous wave walled up and started to barrel over me, and I had a short fast steep ride to the beach. As I wiped out a surfer paddling out said to me, 'You just got in the green room!' That was the nickname for getting inside a tubing wave, but I laughed, as he should have said the brown room! Still smiling from a brilliant wave it clicked; why not call the shop 'the white room,' for the snow? There was, coincidentally, also a good album that my daughter played by KLF, called *The White Room*. That was good enough for me, so I swiftly named the shop 'The White Room.'

I put a board rack on the wall of Clive's hardware shop, a few bits of snow clothing, and a load of stickers, and in true punk style I had a shop! As quickly as I managed to start the shop, I stepped straight into startling shop politics, as Quiksilver immediately supplied me with some clothing. Then, within a week they rang me and said that a surf shop had complained, and now they couldn't supply me any longer! That was the beginning of shop politics that went on for years!

To promote the shop, I excitedly put an amateurish hand drawn advert in *SUK's* third edition, but desperately needed a proper image. I tried ringing Steve, a work colleague from Tunbridge Wells, who was a fabulous doodler, and he absorbed my request. Within a few months Steve had come up with a new logo, and it was just what I had wanted. It captured the feel of the time and was pleasing on the eye; he could have made it as a graphic designer and often sent me doodles. One that he sent me was of a surfer with his feet nailed to his surfboard, which would have overcome the bindings problem! Another great one was a Rasta surfer, called Ijahmansurf, riding a red, gold and green board. So with the logo done the shop felt complete, and a later move to a first floor location in town followed, from where I could sell clothes and boards, without tools and nails!

With the new location the owners covered the working day, but I needed someone to run the shop, as it was all getting too much! Sales just ticked over enough for it to pay its way over the following year, but without having the expertise in the shop during the weekdays it was a drawback, and I couldn't be there often enough. Then like a wish, along came a long blond-haired skater looking for a job!

Simon Maine was in the new school of skating, and a very colourful skate scene was happening in the UK based around streets, ramps and car parks. Simon was happy to work weekdays, but spent weekends in his VW, partying, skating and having fun. He got on with developing the skate side to the shop, while I dealt with the snowboard side. He picked up on the lifestyle and jargon of snowboarding quickly, and we had a good fun relationship. Being in town meant that we had a few thieves, and one day a group of them came in and punched Simon in the face! We also had a lowlife break in to the shop once, and steal the new winter clothing stock just as it had been delivered. Sadly, there was a thick layer of scum over Swansea at that time and there were regular setbacks, so it was not a money-spinner. However, it paid the wages and I could sponsor myself with new boards and boots!

The shop moved twice and ended up at the back of a climbing shop, which was much more suitable. We had a settee and laid-back atmosphere, with a spooky workshop in the ancient basement. The boarders and skaters would come and hang out in the shop, and in the summer evenings we would go wakeboarding down the Mumbles at high tide. We would all chip in to hire a speedboat, and then have a fun session leaping around the bay, and this would be followed by a stroll along the Mumble's mile for a drink or two. They were very good times with a colourful group of characters that enjoyed the laid back aura of the shop. The alternative attraction of the shop had brought them together, creating a special mix in a special time.

For the skaters this was only upset by a new toy in town, which came about from a phone call from Andy Jennings in London. He and his partner, Guy Burnell, had got the licence to import something called a 'Snakeboard.' I had once seen one being used by a pretty German snowboarder in Austria, and she just wiggled her feet, and seemed to propel herself quickly and snake-like very smoothly around a car park. I had been intrigued to understand how it worked, but had never found out, so was excited when Andy sent one down to me. On inspection it looked like the nose and tail of a skateboard that had been cut off, and then joined by a strong plastic spine. The footpads were articulated so that you could swivel your feet, and this swivelling gave the board momentum in short curves, hence the snake name.

One quiet evening I took the board to the council headquarters, which had a smooth tarmac road. My daughter sat and watched me as I struggled to get any coordination, and that was on the flat part of the road. After twenty minutes she innocently said to me, 'I've never seen you crap at anything before!

'That was it, I tried my hardest to get the annoying thing going, frustration and sweat finally got me to the semblance of what I had seen in Austria. It took quite a few sessions to get smooth, and go downhill in control, but I managed it. It did feel a bit like snowboarding, but without that floaty feeling, maybe more like making hard turns on-piste.

We stocked the boards, much to the disgust of the skaters, as all I had to do was sell a box and pads to the young kids that were being rapidly attracted to it. Mothers would come in the shop and buy their kid a board, and the skaters, sat on the settee drinking my coffee, would sneer or look horrified! I just laughed at them, and would take the opportunity to wind them up. 'Skating is dead, you are the new dinosaurs!' was all they could get out of me. Skaters had developed their culture via the streets, and had imperceptible, united principles. Something that I admired and knew was theirs to be lost, if they ever went mainstream. So they always resisted new-fangled wheeled sliding devices, like inline skates or snakeboards, but incredibly, the whole snowboarding thing had been started by the toy-like snurfer!

It also reminded me of the 'skier v snowboarder' rivalry, the established and the new, in conflict. However, as much as I knew that snakeboarding would not takeover skating, it had its place, especially as you could put foot straps on them, which enabled you to make big jumps, in a similar vein to snowboarding. So skateboard tricks had been adapted by snowboarders, now snowboard tricks were being adapted by snakeboarders and some of the youngsters were now pushing it on their snakeboards.

Andy realised that they were more on the toyish side than snowboards were, and was ready to find something better to trade in. So when the importer of Radair snowboards got in to financial difficulties, he took the brand off them, despite not yet snowboarding. Suddenly he had to go to the trade show in Manchester and try and sell snowboards to retailers. He did two things to help himself; firstly he picked people's brains, including mine, and secondly he got a quick artificial face tan, with white panda eyes, to try and look like a pro! Never ceasing to amuse me, he did okay and later moved on to import Osiris skate shoes and Option snowboards from North America, and these brands had a lot more credibility!

Despite all of this going on I was still unable to turn down a new opening, so when Dave Ward Smith, the paraglider, started running snow trips to Peisey Nancroix, near Les Arcs, I started to take a few groups out there with him. The accommodation was situated in a lovely grey stone village, with that timeless rustic feel of a French mountain village bypassed by the modern world. Within a short time of discovering this place, a series of old stone buildings had been purchased by a British flyer that Dave knew, called Pippa. She wanted to split the buildings up into more manageable parts, so I casually told Andy about the buildings, and he got a group together and worked out how to buy one building by dividing the costs into twelfths. So before I knew it I had a twelfth share in an Alpine chalet, as well!

I had achieved nearly everything in snowboarding that I wanted to, and spent many trips going to that wonderful village and valley. We called the chalet 'the Freeride Motel,' and put on training and off-piste trips from there. We did dual paragliding flights with Dave, and would take off from high up in the resort, and then land as near to the chalet as possible, even in the garden! The take off down a steep black run was totally exhilarating, and then the spectacular views followed, across and down the Roseul and Tarentaise valleys. With nothing but air below you, circling the skies like an eagle, gave you an emotional high that left you smiling all night.

— LITTLE SNOW, BIG SNOW —

'Someone has ridden through the race course in
the night and the director is fuming!' –
Eddie Spearing

One day, not long after the Aviemore championships, I took an interesting phone call. It was from Simon, a well-spoken person from Club Ski Andorra. He and his partner, Richard, were interested in running a commercial snowboard trip using our developing network. We chatted over some ideas, and slowly evolved a competition prospect in Pas De La Casa, Andorra. I couldn't face a return trip to Arinsal, after my first insane snow experience. However, Pas looked like a good resort close to the French border, with lashings of reliable snow and sun.

I ran the concept through with the BSA committee as an opportunity to try the British Championships abroad, but they were happy to run them in Aviemore again. In the search for a better venue and facilities, and a free trip abroad, I felt motivated enough to organise an event in Andorra. As the Scottish resorts were not big enough to hold the Super G race I agreed to make the Pas event the official Super G title for that year. The Super G was very fast and potentially dangerous and later dropped from world events, but here was a chance for British riders to compete on European race quality courses. Added to this, I could put on all the events at Pas as well, including the halfpipe. The resort director was offering us whole shebang, even though most events would not count towards the British title.

I figured out that on average there should be more snow in Andorra than Scotland, although Mother Nature does not have hard and fast rules. Despite this, a part of me wondered why I chose to add this to my workload and stress, and I didn't really know? But hey, I would get to be on the mountain and drive around in a piste basher. A pretty good enough reason for me at that time!

The British Championships at Aviemore had been set for 13th to 15th March 1992, and the Pas event was to be from the 4th April 1992. The wheels were set in motion, and we all felt like old hands at organising events by now. It was still worrying for me though, as I wondered how many people would turn up to ensure that Pas would be a success. Particularly worrying were the initial bookings as snowboarders had a habit of doing things as late as possible. Anyhow, as I was not going to go to the Aviemore championships I could fully focus on the Pas competition, and Simon and Richard from Club Ski Andorra were really supportive. They had laid on a good deal for the accommodation and the local slope management were saying the right things. I could see this being a laid back fun time, without much stress, and was cautiously looking forward to it.

I called the Pas event 'The Alpine Cup,' even though it was in the Pyrenees! As the weeks rolled on a few bookings came in and I began to feel better, but it was still below our target to make it worthwhile. We advertised both events in *SUK* and in many snowboard shops, and quite a few of the South Wales local riders had indicated that they would be coming along. As usual, it would be an open event to include anyone, and we expected quite a few overseas riders, and some of the alpine-based Brits that didn't fancy the long trip to Scotland. However, it was a total unknown, and I did have a few sleepless nights over it.

Poor snowfall had plagued the Scottish resorts for a few years, and the Alps had experienced a shocker in 1989. So nowhere was totally sure of good snow, but generally the higher the mountains, the better the chance of snow. Snow canons were used in some resorts, but they were expensive and had limitations. Praying for snow was another option.

Global warming, climate change, fate, or call it what you want, disaster struck Aviemore. In early March, prior to the event, there was absolutely no snow! Eddie waited as long as he could in case new snow arrived, but without a base it would take quite a bit of snow. He rang me in March and said can we turn the Pas event into the full championships? I agreed, but said I would need support, as it was going to be well-subscribed, and probably chaotic. We still did not know how many entrants would come from Europe, but we knew that there would now be a lot from the UK. So from a laid back fun competition this event had suddenly become full on and potentially very stressful.

I had a gut feeling that if this went well it would be difficult for the British Championships to go back to Scotland. I also knew that there were unhappy Scottish locals, as they were used to having the comp in their own backyard. Also the Scottish crew had made history setting up the first two Glenshee contests, and then two more at Aonach Mor and Aviemore with the BSA, so the foundations had been set up for the future. There were a lot of reasons why a British Championships should be on British soil, but I still felt that the facilities of the resorts were not good enough, and that the slope management a bit archaic. Mother Nature also wanted her say in this, and she wasn't playing ball in the UK, so the long-term prospects were not good for reliable snow in Scotland. If the climate change predictions were at all accurate, then it was probably time for change, for better or worse, and I felt vindicated in organising the Pas event, but understood the implications for the locals in Scotland.

There were quite a few frantic phone calls over the weeks before I left, and some surprisingly from foreigners. One such call was from a lovely Kiwi woman, called Vicki, who wanted to go to the event just to watch and was currently in London. I booked her in and said to meet up out there, and I would introduce her to the coterie, at her own risk of course. I had to leave a few weeks earlier to make sure that everything was going to plan, and Eddie armed me with a detailed plan of the halfpipe, including dimensions and various plan views. I left all the other paperwork that would be needed with him, to bring out a few days before the event. All hunky dory!

When I arrived in Pas I was happy to see a good snow base, and a gleaming white resort with blue skies. The main piste ran into the town like a giant tongue, and this made access to the piste very easy, and all of our apartments were based alongside the piste. Fab. I could get up in the morning, step out of the door and ride down to the lift. The locals were very friendly and helpful, and if you stayed in the bar too long you would be plied with free Tequilas! The sun is hotter in Andorra than in the Alps, as it's further south and borders Spain, but this means that the snow melts faster, and that was the only drawback I could see. Horizontal Scottish hailstones or too much sun was the question? I was happy with the latter.

The local riders got involved and the local snowboard shop, Surf Evasio, became a hub of activity, this was going too well. However, the halfpipe was my big concern as this was a new creation on the mountain, and many resorts had never seen one. I badgered the director to start building it as soon as possible so that I could relax and tick that off the big list. He studied Ed's plans and showed me the allotted place for us to build it, and I was given a South American driver and piste basher to work with.

A day later the relaxed hombre and myself started to build the pipe and I sat in the cab directing him from Eddie's plans and now felt glad that we were progressing. On the second day of shovelling huge quantities of snow around we suddenly hit rocks and jumped out of the piste basher to investigate with shovels. It was clear that these rocks were attached to the bedrock, so we tried to shift the pipe across from this obstruction only to find some more of this bedrock the other side. There was damn rock on either side of the centre of our allocated area restricting the width of the halfpipe, making it too narrow to be ridden.

I quickly realised that this particular task was not going to be plain sailing, so I went back to the director again, and he said that there was no other spot to put the halfpipe. I was stumped for the moment, and I sat around it for a few hours thinking through all the options. If we aligned the pipe to one side of the rock, then we could build hits to bypass the narrow neck. It meant that the riders would have to take off from a fixed place on the wall, and not choose their own spot, as preferred. I rang Eddie in the UK and we decided that I would build as much of the pipe as possible, and when the freestylers arrived they could set up the fixed hits where they wanted them.

Despite this annoying problem, I spent another

day in the piste basher and thoroughly enjoyed it, and all the other preparations had gone to plan. Then I had a day off to go riding and having fun before the rest of the BSA cavalry were due to arrive. The racetracks were superb, and the resort staff would run all the races, set the gates and do the timing, and that left the simple matter of registration and communication for us. What could go wrong?

Riders started arriving in Pas from all over Europe, and many new faces were prevalent, and when some of my own local friends arrived I was given a much-needed psychological boost. The atmosphere changed in the resort, as there was now an expectant party feel and the potential of something unique about to happen. I was still concerned about the halfpipe though, and also why the BSA cavalry hadn't arrived yet?

Communication with the others was pretty haphazard by the local landlines in the mobile phoneless world at that time. My last communication from Eddie was that they were about to leave the UK and would arrive yesterday! Very quickly the pressure built as newcomers were demanding to register, and were not used to our laid-back approach, especially the alpine skiers turned snowboarders, who expected professionalism. As I had none of the forms, insurance etc., I put off registration as long as I could, and then I had word that the support team were stuck in Barcelona, and had bought the biggest round ever ordered at the airport, and then had to sleep there! Just before the airport bar closed for the night they ordered one hundred pints of Spanish beer. Yep, this was British snowboarding all right. As it turned out no one had thought about the travel arrangements from the airport to the Pyrenees. Eddie put his Spanish into practice and nearly convinced a local basketball team to share their coach but failed in the end. This meant that I had to keep the whingers at bay, by writing names and events on bits of loose paper and getting part of the job done. When the hungover entourage finally arrived, still in merry spirits, I gave them my choice thoughts!

We quickly got on with the paperwork and then inspected the halfpipe, a small amount of work would resolve the problem, and the freestylers were happy enough to use it. In true British style there was a big party every night, but I was in a nice rhythm from being out there, and paced myself. I had met up with Vicki from New Zealand, and introduced her to Eddie, and before I knew it they were an item. It was turning into a great meeting place for new people to connect with our scene.

The Chamonix crew had brought a Native American with them, who had long dark hair and typical drawn face, and was quite a character. He lived in a hut in Chamonix, and hiked up the mountain for free, instead of paying to use the overpriced lift system. I noticed his unusual looking skis and he proudly showed me these expensive top of the range skis, which had been covered in black spray paint and then scratched. I was taken aback and asked why they looked so tatty.

'Five dollar insurance!' he replied. 'No one is going to steal these skis looking like this.' I had to agree with him, as stealing equipment was a common problem in the big resorts, and to prove his point he left them at the bottom lift every night, and jumped on them first thing in the morning. A host of other colourful people came to the event just for the fun of it and added to the party atmosphere.

With the hasty admin work completed, we finally got the contest started with the Giant Slalom on a well-prepared racetrack, which the efficient Andorrans set the night before ready for the morning. From over one hundred entrants about a third were not British, and they were from all over the planet. Blue sky, recent snow and a good course made for a competitive race, and I was relieved once one event went okay, and that deserving Dutchman, Noel Gaddo, yet again thrashed everyone by four seconds to take the open title. Lloyd Rogers, who was based in St Foy, in the French Alps, took the British title, and had trained very hard for it.

However, the standout for me was Justin Alison, who rode down the course fakie (backwards), and still put in a respectable time. Also, Tony Brown, on being told that helmets were compulsory for the Super G, took to wearing a plastic vegetable colander held on with duck tape. That was the spirit of the time, and it displayed the soul traits that prevailed in snowboarding, bearing in mind many of us had jumped off cliffs or surfed over rocks, without helmets.

Lloyd Rogers went on to win the slalom the next day, and the best performances were by people based overseas, which made it clear that you have to be in reliably snowy mountains to really compete in alpine sports. The dry slope in Scotland can only do so much for your progress, but being overseas left you out of the British scene a bit, and that had proved to be a difficult balance.

Becci Malthouse, another new rider based in the Alps, dominated the women's slalom and giant slalom.

Quite a few Brits were not used to the power of the sun this far south and were getting seriously sunburned, so we suddenly had a load of 'tomato heads,' that made them stand out from the locals. Even chief party organiser, Jeremy Sladen, was glowing in the bar at night, and provided romantic soft lighting for Eddie and Vicki.

The night before the Super G, which was the very event that had kick-started the idea of this competition, there was an even bigger party in town with a DJ. After another bouncing night where the DJ played 'Teen Spirit' for the umpteenth time and Eddie comically raged about it, I headed for bed. Outside in the cold fresh starlit night air, I walked past the bottom of the main piste, and to my surprise Stuart Duncan rode out of the darkness with his board under his arm, sporting a strange look. I was way too merry to wonder what he was doing, and just laughed it off as another Scottish prank.

*

The next morning, after several coffees, I strolled to the race start, and there to greet me was Eddie looking red and agitated with a very perplexed face.

'Someone has ridden through the racecourse in the middle of the night and the director is fuming. He is refusing to hold the race,' he shouted at me.

My brain couldn't take it in. I tried to comprehend what Eddie meant. How could he refuse? Although my brain couldn't understand it, my stomach could, and there was a sinking feeling in the pit of it. The very event I had pinned it all on was now doomed. Was it sabotage, high jinks, or an accident? The director was even more upset as their banners had been damaged as well. Then I remembered the bizarre sighting the night before, a drunken Scotsman, probably on a mission.

I laughed and told Eddie, and he pulled a face as if to say something seriously rude.

'Okay,' I said. 'Let's try again and convince the director to put it on, as we have paid for this and brought customers to their resort'.

Having already seen the director once Eddie wasn't sure that was a viable option, but one of the great things about Eddie is that he can be a charmer, and much slicker than me. I tried to persuade him to give it another go, as so much was riding on this and he slowly came round to it. We went to see him again, and Eddie pulled his best sad face, and sweet-talked him around within half an hour, but it wasn't easy. The egg was off my face! But, hey this was snowboarding, not skiing, and I loved it.

When the Super G finally started, I watched from the bottom of the track to be able to see a lot of the action. Then I realised I had nothing to do as the Andorrans were running the race smoothly, and a few BSA helpers were mucking in at the top. I walked away from the track towards the town, and sat and watched from a distance as the little human dots sped down the pristine white racetrack at high speed. It looked amazing from where I was, but I had a bittersweet feeling. I felt slightly detached from it, as if it was a child leaving home, and despite the problems that we had encountered, things were moving on in an irreversible direction. For better or worse, again!

Needless to say Noel Gaddo won the open title with another blistering performance from the 'Flying Dutchman'. The alpine-based Brits did best with newcomer Neil McNab first, but for me the standout performance was from a stressed out, hung over Eddie Spearing, coming thirteenth on this massive course. It was a great relief when the event was finally over. I celebrated with a lovely coffee in the hot sun. I sat in the afternoon melancholy and watched snow melting on the rooftops of the tall buildings, and then plummeting to the streets below with a thud. The waiters ran in and out of the door quickly, just in case they were caught in a sudden fall of wet snow. I liked this simplicity and laid-back way of living, and I couldn't help comparing it to

Aviemordor, which now seemed like a dark, faraway place. Pinning your whole event on the weather conditions had proved to be stressful at the best of times, but Pas had come up with the goods.

The competing freestyle hardcore riders were being turned on by the new school wave of trick riding, which had recently developed in America. Urban skate moves were being done on snowboards; the era of 'jibbing' had arrived. From the development of skate parks with bowls in the seventies, to the aggressive street skating that later evolved, skating assimilated the streets and city obstacles as challenges. This was transferred into snowboarding, and snow parks were being created with obstacles to jump on, over or slide along. It was a new aspect to snowboarding that had never been dreamed of in the early days, and wasn't particularly cool with soul riders. It was, however, cool with city skaters and rebels, and along with it came the baggy clothes, hip-hop played loud, graffiti and more attitude.

Not to be out done, and with so many photographers about, the Brits proceeded to ride around the town. There were patches of snow spread around the streets so they rode down steps, handrails, off walls and even jumped off snowy telephone boxes and balconies. This was something new for the locals, and a taste of American future trends. The locals found it very amusing, and didn't have any problem with it, which was a surprise, but then they were so laid-back and enjoyed life to the full. I know that some places would have called the cops and made a big scene out of it.

The following day, we had good snow and blue sky for the halfpipe event – a photographer's dream. There were fewer entrants than for the racing as some were intimidated going up against the top group of freestylers. About forty entered this hard fought contest that showcased the progress made by British boarders over the last few years. The airs were now slicker and smoother and more complicated, so judging them was also more difficult, and we were moving onto another level. Although the girls competed in the halfpipe, they didn't display the same aggression and big air that the men executed.

Despite the constraints of the rock bed, that forced the hits to be at certain points, they still put on a great show. The pipe should have been better, but halfpipes were still developing, and took a lot of work, as we had found out over recent years. I had nothing to do but watch and enjoy the spectacle, so I had my trusty Nikonos underwater camera with me, and I snapped the riders as close as possible.

I managed to get a beautiful shot of Chod, poised high above the pipe, with blue sky and white snow in the background. Eddie and Stig put the shot on the magazine cover of their sixth edition of *SUK*, and as Chod went on to win the overall British title it was fitting and summed up the event for me. Justin Allison won the freestyle and Simon Smith took a close second place. We had run a juniors event as well and Peyton Burnett and Richard Stephenson, from the Swansea slope, did very well.

The usual tongue in cheek award ceremony took place, followed by the very usual party.

This had been a fun event and allowed the serious boarders to compete in good conditions, while a lot of new faces had appeared on our scene and the next wave of ski boarders and snowboarders was happening. The lifestyle was slowly becoming more of a sport, and some riders had clearly done a lot of training. Before we even left Andorra, there were murmurings about the next British Championships being abroad.

From this event the best riders available had to rush straight to Avoriaz, in the French Alps, to represent Britain in the Nations Cup, a team event. However, the freestylers fell asleep in a lay-by on the autoroute, and were consequently late, so they were ribbed by the Euros as Brits that drunk too much beer! And so our reputation remained intact in the rest of Europe.

Eddie, Jeremy and the Scottish crew took the difficult route back to Barcelona airport again, but most of us took the easy route home.

CHAPTER EIGHTEEN — 1993 to 1996

— MOVIN' ON —

*'If the Ocean is the Mother I never knew, then
the Mountains are the Father I never knew.'*

By 1993 there was a rhythm to the UK snowboard world. The BSA and *SUK* magazine were on a roll with exciting happenings, events and courses. These were heady times to be involved in snowboarding, and the effort put in by the people involved had provided a foundation to promote this culture. The trade better understood that this was not skiing, and despite the ongoing antagonism between skiing and boarding, a sensitive healthy gap existed.

SUK had established a fabulous annual board test, which was a raucous opportunity to test next year's new boards, with their ever-changing, go higher and go faster, hi-tech innovations. It was also summer boarding on the glaciers, so sometimes you could sleep under the stars or party in the road. When Eddie and Stig started *SUK* the most crucial article in the first issue was a board test. They managed to go to Austria to test boards, along with American pro-skater and snowboard innovator, Rob Morrow, as they were being paid by the Daily Mail to write up the event for the *Daily Mail* Great British

Ski Week. They hastily produced their board test results and published them in *SUK*, before the *Daily Mail* put theirs out to the public. That ended their relationship with the *Daily Mail*, and anyway the board test atmosphere would have grated on the skiers and the *Daily Mail*, so the board test evolved in the hands of snowboarders.

In the UK the summer dry slope competition series was growing, becoming an institution for great freestyle and parties. These events became launching pads for new videos and clothing ranges, while music and fashion affixed themselves to the rolling series. They became a complete entity of snow culture in the cities, but without the snow, due to the fairly unique situation in the UK with summer plastic boarding. It was a vibrant, fun time with great potential for the future.

Along with the competition series, most of the dry slope instructors training courses were run out of the winter season, when the slopes were quieter. The demand for them grew and grew and by now we had trained instructors to run the courses in various parts of the country. The slopes that had accepted boarding were developing as busy regional centres.

At Swansea slope we now had a good teaching team with Evo, Ron and Mary trained up and covering the influx of new boarders, and creating an energetic atmosphere. These centres were also producing a new generation of riders, mainly attracted through magazines and media coverage. This next wave of young riders learned fast and pushed the air tricks to another level, as what was once very difficult to learn became the norm. A phenomenon that is seen in many sports, when an instantaneous spread of a new trick travels across the world, and mind barriers are broken before your very eyes.

However from the dark recesses of the minds of the Scottish crew came another movement. When I first saw the advert in *SUK* I was surprised and slightly annoyed. It was headed SAD, and it said, 'Dendex sucks. Do you?' Jealousy, bigotry or were they just being complete wind-up merchants, who knew? SAD stood for 'Snowboarders Against Dendex,' rather than some seasonal complaint. I gradually saw the funny side of it though, as I spent too much time on Dendix, and they couldn't even spell it right! SAD ran for some time and encapsulated the self-deprecation and anarchical nature of the innards of snowboard culture.

On the other hand, the general media were responsible for the overblown glamorised image of snowboarding, portraying a rebellious lifestyle, and consistently linking it to almost anything. The *Daily Mail* was regularly outspoken against snowboarding, and appeared to enjoy the controversy, especially in its newspaper circulation, and even demanded the ban of this 'killer craze.' The undercurrent from influential skiers was still clearly anti-snowboarding, although the financial aspect was turning heads and causing divisions within the ski world. The snippets of news, fake or not, and hearsay were constant and the public didn't yet have the Internet to search out the truth. The media also had a habit of turning alternative culture into mainstream, by attracting business, advertisers and 'sofa' people into it. The eventual outcome would probably be a watered down façade of the original culture, and although that would take time, the cracks were just becoming visible from the heart of the snowboard world.

The media managed to attract new riders to slopes that didn't have the same spirit and skills as the early riders, and this meant that we had to respond accordingly in our teaching methods. Some debutants were turning up at the slopes with the belief that snowboarding was very easy to learn and very trendy. They expected to be riding fast and flying through the air just like they had witnessed on their TV screens or in the media.

The snowboard trade was now in a groove, and they had to order their product in the spring for the following winter, which meant that they had to get all the samples to the annual trade show held in Manchester, at the G-MEX exhibition centre. The trade stands were generally snowboard only or ski only, with some accessory stands being of interest to all retail outlets. This annual stock purchasing for shops became another big party where all the buyers were 'wined and dined,' but at the same time the shop owners had to predict sales for the following season, and put their money on the line. It was difficult to do, but as the sales were generally moving upwards it was usually a case of selling more. The complexity of the task was the ever-increasing new brands and gimmicks, and forecasting which brands would the riders want to get their hands on. However, Manchester was a fun place to visit and had its own unique atmosphere. On my first trip I entered a lift in a posh hotel and heard totally unexpected techno music coming out of the speakers!

Then there was Manchester's China town, which was a great place to binge eat in the night, especially after spending the day walking miles around the stands. Keeping a track on how much stock you ordered sent your head into a spin, but if you got lucky, one of the importers of skate and snow stuff, like Shiner, would take you for a twenty-course Chinese gourmet experience and several Tsingtaos.

It was around the third time that I had made my annual trip there to order the stock for the shop, and it was getting routine and predictable, so I knew what to expect. I strolled in to the big G-MEX hall ready for a look at next year's snowboard offerings, but what greeted me shocked me to the core. Mixed in between random flouro ski companies clobber were dark, dark snowboard stands. It was yin and yang as I stood in shock for a few minutes to take it in, while my brain struggled with the complete lack of colour in the snowboard areas.

I finally went into a dark snowboard stand and requested some explanation; 'What the hell is going on?' I queried. 'Next year's image!' came the smirky

194

reply.

I looked at all the clothing, and it was dark green, dark aubergine, dark blue or black, and any inkling of bright colour had been completely sucked out of the glad rags. I sat down and gratefully accepted a coffee, wondering how the hell I was going to sell this stuff next year, as it was my hard earned money in jeopardy. We chatted for a while, and then I wandered around the rest of the show to absorb it all.

What I saw was all the snowboard brands, except for a few from Europe had gone dark. This left the skiing fraternity looking on in bewilderment, but as I strolled I began to see it, finally the clothing for snowboarding was snowboarding. No more mish-mash of colours and styles, as dark and baggy would proclaim who boarders were, and it was heavily skate influenced. A sort of uniform of freedom I guessed, but freedom from what I didn't know? Maybe the skiing fraternity, who just couldn't assimilate this sea change.

I inspected the clothing at each stand and it was all fully functional for boarding, even though we could all end up looking like we were going fishing instead of snowboarding. I just secretly hoped that it was going to sell next year, but in many ways it was a brilliant coup, and the ski clothing soon looked very dated after spending a few days in the hall. Tight and flouro was definitely dinosaur now, so the divide between skiers and boarders had taken a new twist.

Around this time there was a growing movement

amongst the shops selling boards and technical clothing in the UK. As the sport expanded, so did the outlets trying to sell boards. However, it took some expertise to get the appropriate equipment for each individual. Stories of people being sold unsuitable boards and boots, from random shops, were getting more common. The stores that were run by people that actually boarded felt that they had to stand up and say something. So someone came up with an advert idea that listed these shops under the name 'BOSS.' This stood for Boarder Owned Snowboard Shops, and it was based on an earlier movement, called 'SOS,' which stood for 'Skater Owned Shop.' We were trying to keep the expertise and soul of boarding in the sales arena too. This was before the Internet became popular of course, but it worked to a degree, and gave the serious shops credibility, and the assurance of a professional service.

In the mountain resorts specialist snowboard shops had sprung up, often started by the local snowboard hero. So most visiting boarders would head there for spares, or to get good local information on where to ride and where to drink in the evening. These shops understood our needs better and usually had cool staff to chat to, and were preferable to the big ski chain stores that dominated the mountains, and were full of clumping skiers, inadvertently poking you with their sticks or skis.

In the early years I used to frequent the 'Sweet Snow Surf Shop,' in Tignes, France, where the owner, Dennis Leroy, was very helpful, and a full-on character. He was fearless on the mountain, and had become the French Snowboard mogul champion, with his head on, brain out approach.

He didn't need much encouragement to take time out and show me some hidden secret spots.. On one such day he got away late from the shop, so we stayed up the mountain after the lifts closed to take some dramatic photos. He rode through the avalanche barriers at high speed, and then he hit a huge snow lip to get air in the evening sunset. It was a heart-stopping moment of awesome beauty, tinged with danger, and then we had the rest of the deserted mountain to ride down through the orange-tinted snow, twisting and turning like swallows at sunset. We always finished off a perfect time with a 'biere et picon,' in the Snooker Bar, with Jacqui, the owner, and that encapsulated the beauty of local boarder owned shops.

Another legendary French snowboard shop that opened around 1990, was 'Tip Top,' in Bourg St Maurice, which had its' roots in the film *Apocalypse Snow*, and served an amazing area that included Les Arcs, St Foy, La Rosiere and more. The shop staff helped many Brits over the years with guiding, teaching and equipment, and made for a good excuse to drop down from the resorts and sample local life.

So the pulse of '90s British boarding happily skimmed above the splintered general society that was trying to pay the rent and party, but there were dark clouds looming on the distant horizon. Some of us had occasional sleepless nights, thinking about potential approaching problems, and in the mid '90s one issue pointed to the changing future.

A customer came in the White Room and took advice on the best board for their use. Without buying anything they left, and weeks later I saw the person on the local slope with the recommended board purchased off the new-fangled Internet. This gave me a bad feeling for the future of small local shops in these specialised products, if the Internet became popular over the long-term.

Jake Burton, in the USA, was always aware that the big ski manufacturers could try to take over board production. I was aware that the ski bodies could try and take over our teaching system, and competition, even though the ski council in Wales had already given assurances that this would not happen, and that the British Ski Council had absolutely no interest in snowboarding. There was, however, also a body in Britain that ran ski instructor training, called BASI, and rumours circulated that they wanted to run snowboard teaching. So generally, the biggest threat to the blooming snowboard scene was either the Internet, or the skiing fraternity.

Snowboarders links to the underground hardcore hip-hop, street skate culture, and the need to constantly change could easily have become its undoing. There was a constant internal battle between being sucked into stupidity by some elements, and being cloned into skiing by others.

Competitions, magazines and cliques were where the influences were being asserted, pushing and pulling the shape of snowboarding. In fact, snowboarding was losing sight of its roots and soul, however, it also made for a prickly ball for the skiing bodies to deal with; a double-edged sword. Although one thing was definitely for sure; snowboarding was here to stay, and the doubters were wrong! Snowboarding was being swept along on a wave of energy, fashion, mags, music, culture and competition. Mother Nature provided our playground, freedom from rules our guiding light and civilisation our viands, and this crazy fusion, much like our spinning planet, had no one fully in control of its direction!

CHAPTER NINETEEN — 1994

— INSIDE OUT —

'Split the mountain with the edge of your hand,
and make a playground in paradise land.'

In the early days, when Dave Furneau started using the dry slope at Ackers Trust in Birmingham, he dropped a board in for the staff to use. However, it had no bindings on it, so ski instructor, Marc Chester, learned to ride it down the slope without any bindings! Dave later dropped some off for him, and with that big benefit Marc was set on a career in snowboarding.

Marc developed the slope into a high quality snowboard centre, and he learned to race and compete in freestyle off the ramps, achieving some impressive results over the years. He supported the roots snowboard philosophy, and he went on to develop a snowboard team that did displays around the country. Along with Danny Wheeler and Aaron Jennings, they named their radical demonstration team, the 'Team Extreme'. Marc spent some years displaying and running the snowboard teaching at Ackers, until a great opportunity opened up for him.

For some years before, there had been rumours circulating of a small indoor snow slope being built in the Telford area, and it turned out to be a private venture based on an idea developed in Adelaide. Indoor snow, marketed under the name 'Pro Snow,' was produced and laid on a very small experimental slope. This idea slowly turned into a commercial reality, when a large warehouse-type fridge was built in Tamworth, with a complex attached that included the slope, a leisure pool, shops and restaurants.

As it was being developed the rumours ran rife, but in the end a 170-metre slope was opened with a conveyor belt along the side to get you to the top. And guess what? Snowboarders were banned! So in 1994 the first commercial indoor snow slope opened in the UK, and banned snowboarders immediately. Marc was offered a job at the new 'Snowdome,' and knew that it was only a matter of time before they would need the income from snowboarders to get by. Eddie from *SUK* worked hard to convince the blinkered management to allow boarders on, and after six months we had access to this novel snow strip.

Marc developed the teaching there, using our courses, and made it a commercial and fashionable success. He also set up a snowboard night, which was called 'Board Stiff,' that had ramps, great music, and a party in the bar immediately after the fun on the slope, it became very popular and served the Midlands and beyond.

I would sometimes hire a minibus and run trips there for the local boarders in Swansea to sample this taste of the future. It was always exciting arriving in the car park in the summer, knowing that you were going to be riding on the white stuff, out of season. By white stuff, I mean that the snow was some form of ice, and while being far from powder it was totally acceptable. I guess that I would describe it as similar to a firm piste in a winter resort, but as a teaching arena, and as a place to improve yourself, ready for your trip to the mountains, it was great. The cold temperature inside the warehouse gave you that Alpine feeling, and as a board-testing venue it was much better than a plastic dry slope, so Eddie was quickly on to this! We also realised that we could also use the Snowdome as a meeting place for the BSA, and then go for a board afterwards. It also became a place for special events and parties, and was undoubtedly an important location in the development of British snowboarding.

It was a difficult business to run though, so it went through some changes of ownership, but it set the scene for the future. The costs to set up and run one of these installations were inevitably high, and it wasn't many years before different snow systems were developed, and more indoor snow experiences spread here and abroad. Some of them have even been built in very hot countries, like India and Dubai, and this is one future for snow lovers, however to me it's still not as good as the real thing! Perhaps a vast one should have built in the Cairngorms, to keep out that perishing wind and retain the precious snow!

CHAPTER TWENTY — 1993 to 1995

— LEARN TO LOVE
AGAIN, AND AGAIN —

'Delicate snowflakes dream up vast avalanches.'

Some years after I had learned to surf I had a dream that I was sat floating on my surfboard as usual, but now it was amongst well-spaced out trees, on a boundless, surreal plane of glassy water. Whenever the thunderous sound of an approaching wave rolled through the woods, my senses sharpened up ready to predict the sudden appearance of a shiny wall of water coming through the trees. I had to paddle furiously on its approach, then after an endless slow motion take off down the reflective, glassy wall of water I would carve turns between the trees at high speed. It was crazy and wild, but I loved it. Primal ocean spirit!

Years later, I did exactly the same riding through powder snow in the real trees, but this time on a snowboard, and the dream just popped back into my head during the ride. I realised that on the right board in the right conditions, it was easy to forget whether you were snowboarding, or surfing, or even having a surreal dream!

Jeremy Sladen, that perennial purveyor of snowboard equipment, was never far from what I was doing, and on one of our get togethers took the opportunity to off-load some surplus snowboard equipment on me. Like a magician, he produced the strangest looking board from his enormous bag of stuff. What appeared to be a rocket-shaped board was made by the American company Nitro, and was coloured the purple side of blue, and at 1.96m long was far longer than the average board. The sharp pointed nose and swallowtail were distinct traits from surfing and the early snowboards, but this was much longer and narrower than I had previously witnessed.

Jeremy's slick sales patter speedily sold me the board, although we both knew that I really wanted it from the glazed look in my eyes. I had loved my first real Sims board that had subtler design traits than this Nitro displayed, so maybe I thought I could have some fun on this new machine. As it was, the average new board design by the main brands had become restricted into smaller, subtle changes; so trying something quite radical could well be the stimulating challenge that I unconsciously needed.

The next opportunity that I had to try out this crazy looking board on the mountain came out of the blue. I had to go to a snow instructor's course being run in Avoriaz in the French Alps. Martin Drayton was organising the course at 'Chalet Snowboard.' Ian Trotter and Gillian Hall had started this chalet holiday company, originally based in Serre Chevalier, and their image was founded on the needs of snowboarders only, to give them a real alternative to 'ski' holiday attitudes. A wise business move took them to Avoriaz later on, and although I was not a fan of the weird architecture in Avoriaz, a huge number of Brits went there every winter. Ian was also an advocate of hard boots and carving boards, and in an interview in the first edition of *SUK* magazine was quoted as saying, 'hard boots for hard men,' which seemed to follow him for years. Both he and Gillian were good racers, and did well over the years in British comps, and as the chalet expanded it became a Burton board test centre, and many good boarders passed through their happy doors.

Eddie wanted me to go on this course to keep a connection between the snow and dry slope courses, but my heart was not totally in it for various reasons. However, I strangely found something that I had been unknowingly looking for – a gift of an unknown thing maybe, or finding love in a dark place. Was it that pinball of life again?

On arrival in Avoriaz, I quickly grabbed the opportunity to try out the Nitro powder dart, as there was evidently some good off-piste to be had. After catching a laborious series of lifts, I finally took off with mixed anticipation and had to ride down a few firm pistes, sketchily turning the board. The initial verdict was that it certainly wouldn't carve, but made acceptable skidded turns, so I experimented with weight shifts to try and find a sweet spot. I quickly discovered that I had to react quickly to this twitchy board or I would be on the rocks.

Then I discovered a good bit of off-piste – with untouched powder – and I let the board go and tried to adjust to it quickly. It floated and floated, just like in my wet woody dream, and the narrow nose and swallowtail allowed me to cut sharp turns, and I could go anywhere with style and flotation. This was a revelation and it was a great feeling, and much better than the standard lollipop shaped boards, which were really a compromised shape. I was ecstatic!

While I was cruising through the soft stuff it suddenly dawned on me that this feeling must have been the same for those early riders that used the toy snurfer. Even though snurfers were so basic in good powder, they would give you exactly the same floaty feeling, and turn easily and precisely, so no wonder Jake Burton got hooked!

After a few hours of exciting off-piste, I was slipping into over confidence, especially when I went back on to the firmer pistes. The board was suddenly edgy and skiddy on piste, and I was also tight for time to get back to the start of the training course. So, in my haste, I took the direct route through a new snowboard park, which served the freestylers and new wave jibbers, and had obstacles to jump on or slide along, spread thoughtfully around the park. I spotted a large picnic table approaching, so I cockily ollied the board high to make sure that I didn't ride into the table. I managed to gain enough height, but I hadn't seen that the table was covered in a fairly thick sheet of ice. The board briefly landed on the table and swiftly skidded me into a backward somersault. Both the nose of the board, and my nose, took all the impact on the rock hard icy floor below!

I slowly worked my way down to a descending lift, with a bloody nose, and a board with a snapped nose. The lift was broken and there was no other way down the cliff face, so I had gone from ecstasy to agony in hours. Then, when I finally got in the chalet, I met one of the course attendees, Lou Currie. She fleetingly looked at the board and said, 'That's a toy, you want to come to Serre Chevalier and see a Swell Panik!' I was slightly offended but also intrigued, despite my painful fat nose.

Lou was tall, athletic, pretty and blonde, and not only that, she could board very well, so every opportunity we had I would quiz her about these utopian boards. Not only did she own a Swell Panik, but she was also a close friend to the creator of them, the mysteriously named 'Kafi,' a mysterious name to affix to my developing mysterious deviation. By the end of the course week, I had learned a lot about the boards that Kafi made under the name of 'Swell Panik.' These boards were unusually handmade, and being a surfer I had definitely experienced swell panic, many times, so I could relate to the name.

I was hooked and my curiosity roused. If she was right and this board would outperform the Nitro ride, and could be carved like a race board on piste, then I had stumbled into something pretty special. I trusted Lou, but worried that she was just exaggerating a bit, so I went back to the UK to cool off, but I struggled to stop thinking about the swallowtail encounter. The Nitro was truly trashed on its first outing and only fit for the bin, but my nose and ego had quickly healed.

On my next visit to the chalet near Les Arcs, France, this burning curiosity got the better of me, so I contacted Lou, and she agreed to take me to see Kafi. I overcame my vow never to go back to Serre Chevalier, after that lift ticket disaster in the early days. Taking off in the icy early hours one dark, cold morning, I drove out of the Alps from one valley, southwards along the flat autoroute, and back in another winding valley to Serre Che, to meet Lou and her partner, Olivier. Olivier rode a Swell Panik everywhere, and was a true mountain man that made his living from teaching sports in the mountains. After that further confirmation, I decided that there was a good chance that I would buy a board.

Yet another valley drive took us to a little stone village, near Briancon, to meet up with Kafi in an intriguing new locality for me. It felt like a strange journey into local's lives that tourists did not normally experience. On our arrival Kafi stood tall, dark and strong, framed in the doorway of his workshop. He was a big character in all ways, and spoke very good English, amongst many other languages. He warmly showed me how he made the boards with a press that he had designed himself, and how every part of the process was done to perfection. He stored the wood, metal etc. at the optimum temperature and humidity, and then he glued the boards together at the perfect pressure and temperature. He had spent years perfecting these tolerances, and in particular the shapes and the proportions of the board.

He gleaned feedback from local riders, and tested the boards himself at La Grave, the famous steep off-piste resort. He told me that he had worked on the side cut and flex for years, and that at last it was now homogenous! In short this man was a genius. He had stayed with the original shapes like the Winterstick, and perfected them rather than compromising and making the typical all-round board. There was a local cult following that used the boards to ride serious off-piste, but some even raced them through slalom courses. His earliest boards were still going strong, despite being well used, and there was no comparison between his board manufacturing and the factory produced boards that nearly all snowboard companies marketed. His slogan that was usually printed on his boards said 'Ride with Pride.'

In those days Kafi rode in hard boots and bindings, as this was partly because of the culture in France at that time. Also, Lou told me that Kafi would be first at the lift in La Grave if it snowed, and he was so hyper that no one could talk to him. On reaching the summit, he would click his feet in quicker than someone in soft bindings, and be first to make tracks down the very steep mountain. That was his commitment to achieving perfection, from making his own boards, to riding them down the mountain. When he was forced to ride on piste he also found that hard boots and bindings were better for carving and speed.

At the end of my guided tour Kafi informed me that he had sold nearly all of his new boards, but had one left out of that year's output. The core of the board was made of Ash, and he had put a sheet of Maple wood on the top of this one. It wasn't attractive like the boards made in the style of early wooden surfboards with inlaid strips of differing woods, but I had little choice. As he generally took off to Chile for some big wave surfing after a long winter, I quickly snapped up his last board, after all it was the performance that I wanted rather than the look. His personal boards were beautiful works of art, and would have made amazing tabletops or mantle pieces! I was told to give the board a name and to get ready for an amazing experience, and hopefully that floating feeling again. I took his advice to ride with hard boots and bindings as I was used to them, and he set it up with my hard bindings firmly drilled into the well-varnished wood. As my own shop was sponsoring me I parted with the cash, and walked away very happy, but I had still not ridden one! I'd just done hell of a lot of talking about them, thinking about them, and now looking at them.

Back in Les Arcs, Malcolm and friends were ripping up the mountain. I drove back to them in the dropping light, after saying thanks and farewell to Lou. After a while I passed La Grave, and again looked at the impossible steepness of it from the road. I remembered that Just Ski coach journey past here some years previously and it was now my mission to snowboard there one day, but three hours later I was back up the mountain in Peisey Nancroix Nancroix, a satellite village in Les Arcs. My new board was searing tracks through my mind, and its 185 cm length caused a lot of comments from the others in the chalet, and a raucous piss-take took place. But I went to bed happy, although I could not sleep too well due to the excitement of trying out this new speed machine the next day.

In the morning the sun shone, and we had a deep blue sky contrasting against the glaring white snow. We took the Trans Arc and got on to the huge peak of Aguille Rouge. At over 10,000 feet (3200 metres) there had to be some powder leftovers that were hard to get to. We rode the pistes for half an hour as the edges were tracked out, and I had to readjust my style of riding a bit, but the board was very fast.

Every time I relaxed it accelerated, and I had to get in control of it, much like a race board. The internal core of this deceptive machine was really a race board, and it was streets above how the Nitro had performed on piste.

From the bottom of the peak I saw the telltale spray of boarders riding deep powder. They had hiked to a steep face that had been partially dynamited by the avalanche safety team and I knew that's where I needed to be. We took off in search of powder, and once up there via several lifts a short hike took us to a wind lip, and a quick clamber got us to the avalanche that was far bigger than it appeared from below. We rode slowly across the chunky avalanche to reach a beautiful steep, deep powder field.

I rested high above the purpose-built town of Les Arcs 2000. It looked like an ants nest far below as little dark dots slid across the white desert. I waited with some apprehension as my breathing recovered in the thin, cold air. I tried to appreciate the stunning views, but the potential of dropping in on this snowfield was causing my stomach to churn. My twitching body could wait no more and I finally jumped around and went straight for a few metres, then the board floated on the powder; the turns came without effort or conscious rotation. Strangely, I felt as if I already knew this board from surfing! I cranked hard turns, so that my face was inches from the snow slope, and I caught glimpses of the spray flying out on each turn as they were quickly left behind. I was floating and flying down this magnificent mountain, and my spirit was soaring again, just like surfing in Constantine all those years ago. This was a climax in snowboarding highs for me – the board, mountain and myself had blended into one for a moment! I didn't need to adjust my riding style, as the balance of the board was perfect in powder, and this was undoubtedly the best board I had ever ridden, and I had successfully sponsored myself to happiness! As I rode, a thought briefly crossed my mind that Kafi had put a bit of his soul into each board that he had made.

Once back at the chalet, after a long day's riding, I sat smiling, drinking tea and indulging in freshly baked chalet cake. The boys were not taking the piss anymore, and they had struggled to keep up with this flying machine on or off piste. It had matched my big expectations to my surprise, and the feeling that I had for this board was pretty special. It was not like the love of another person that could be slowly engulfed either in indifference or hatred, but the love of an object that gave you a high performance beyond ephemeral fashion. We were like two bits of a jigsaw, never yet met but finally put together by accident or fate; it was love at first ride!

My sanctimonious boycott of Serre Che fell apart, as I went back many times over the years. I even swallowed my pride and bought a lift pass. But, in times of good snow it has fabulous terrain that I didn't experience on the first visit there, and I was also drawn to Lou, Kafi and Swell Panik, and also the mesmerizing mountain of La Grave, which had tantalizingly touched my dreams.

I went back to interview Kafi on exactly how he made his boards, and consequently produced an article for *SUK* magazine. I spent the whole day and evening with him getting all the facts right. I learned so much for myself at the same time. It was a great opportunity for me, and then over a really good evening meal and a few drinks, he suggested that we test some boards the next day.

Bleary-eyed we met up the next morning and

rode around the back bowls of Serre Che, and he showed me a myriad of hidden stashes of good powder that I would never have found on my own. His riding technique displayed his years of experience riding these amazing powder machines, even on the occasional cruddy and crusted slopes. I could now see how far these boards could be pushed in differing conditions, and it inspired me to push my limits further than I had been. We ended the day in a café in La Salle, close to the Lievre Blanc, where I had been many years before on the snowboard camp, legs totally exhausted and feeling completely satisfied.

That same week Lou suggested that we visit La Grave, as fresh snow was due. I was simultaneously happy and apprehensive. La Grave village, a typical stone built farming community, hugged the steeply rising sides close to the floor of the Romanche Valley. The 'White Gold' of skiing brought a superior winter income to this valley, like it had to most of the valleys of the Alps. The mainly south facing village looks across and up to the steep icy cliffs that lead further up to the impressive La Meije pinnacle. Often called 'Her Majesty', she is a sharp peak reaching 3,984 metres (13,071 feet) that dominates the slopes of steep glacial snowfields, couloirs and crevasses below. Although this peak has been traditionally treated as feminine, it undoubtedly struck me that it was more like a stern, but good-looking father figure that was capable of dishing out severe punishment. However, whichever sex it was, I was now in its royal court and making a mistake here could be a costly error.

The only lift up this snowy steepness was old, and had originally been built for tourists to view the glacier and seracs at the top. As there were no official pistes coming back down to the bottom, there was not a proper ski patrol, and the usual security of a ski resort. So basically you were on your own, which suited me as I prefer to know that I have to try and get out of the shit that I create. It has been a 'paradise of extremes, due to severe avalanches, hidden crevasses and steep rocky slopes, with an awe-inspiring reputation that goes before it, along with the many tales of serious injuries and death that swirl around the area. There are many unfortunate accidents that happen all over the Alps every year, but the ratio of users to severe incidents have been higher at La Grave. It's not generally frequented by holiday skiers, and is really only suited to advanced riders, or guided tours. Therefore only a handful of people go there, and if the conditions are icy it is undoubtedly a place to avoid.

So, on a blue-sky day, we drove along the picturesque winding valley through the Col de Lautaret to La Grave and took vein-pumping expressos in the ramshackle village café. Lou and I were both armed with Swell Paniks and clambered in to one of the rickety bubble cars of the famed string that went steeply up the mountain. Inside the cabin, above some wise looking graffiti that I couldn't translate, was a cartoon sticker simply indicating that the planet was dying, an auspicious start. The concealed scenery unfolded as we progressed up the lower steepness, and revealed a seriously beautiful place, with La Meije always looking imposingly over it all. Lou pointed out the three couloirs called Les Trifides, the first a banana shape, the second was straight, and the third needed a freefall jump to reach it and luckily was another straight one. I suddenly felt slightly terrified, with my fragile skin and bones very vulnerable in this harsh but beautiful landscape. However, as I was spending much more time off piste than on it, I really wanted this challenge.

The lift was now hundreds of feet above the ground, and Lou nonchalantly opened the door to get an unobstructed view. Stupidly, I looked down and my head span like a top with so much air beneath us, and the bubble cars suddenly felt so flimsy. We then passed over a dividing ridge and the ground moved much closer. Then as we approached the top of the resort, the Dome came into view and I felt relieved to get on to 'terra firma.' I surveyed the wonderful ice cliffs with pale blue strata, layered like limestone. I became mesmerised by these sublime shades of pale blue colours. In recent years I liked to look out for these special colours concealed in ice lips and snow faces. Here there were plenty of these subtle gems to stare at in awe, and the whole glacier was absolutely stunning with its distorted ice blocks, seracs, crevasses and dimpled snow cover. It was breathtaking, and all fear had instantly departed from me to be replaced with wonder. We had to sit down and take it all in for its insane beauty.

We decided to get the easy T-bar over the glacier, and ride along the top of the ice cliffs, so that I could get some photos of it all. We hiked to get in position, and then I rode first, working my way around a beautiful ice cliff to get in position for a shot. I signalled to Lou that I was ready and she rode fast across the top firing spray turns, while I took photos. As she quickly approached the cliff edge, I suddenly had visions of her going over it. I jumped up waving madly and she pulled up close to the icy drop, thankfully. What an amazing place for taking dramatic pictures! I could have spent all day there in the changing light, but we had some big descents to attempt.

To the left of the large ridge we had ascended lay a huge powder field, temptingly in front of us, but riskily strewn with hidden crevasses, and the telltale lumps in the snow that often indicated deep cracks in the glacial ice below. As we sat on the glacier surveying any recent riders tracks that would assist our planned route, a noise came from nowhere, much like a stone sliding across ice. But it was everywhere at once, and the floor shuddered under my buttocks. Wow! That was the first time I had ever felt a glacier move, and another fear chill went through me. This was serious, and my senses sharpened up suddenly. I was acutely aware of the fragile nature of this environment and the need to ride a fine line, and in being fully focused.

We started the descent by dropping down a fantastic steep powder slope, and accelerated very quickly. Then the terrain levelled out a bit to where the crevasses lay in waiting. We tried to stay fairly close to the previous tracks laid down by some earlier riders. I felt the wind resistance on my face change as my speed increased to very fast, and I could feel the solid air shaping my cheeks. I had never been this fast before, and I was forced to make gentle, arching turns, and look well ahead for lumps and banks.

At this speed I could not afford to make any sudden movements in case of speed wobble. I went very still and deep inside myself while travelling at these motorway velocities.

Large plumes of powder spray were just visible out of the corner of my eyes, but I didn't dare look at them for fear of falling off. The board handled the speed very well, with just a bit of slapping on some dimpled bits, but that thought of digging the nose in, and rag dolling into a crevasse, kept me fully attentive. The huge open area was quickly eaten up, after screaming across it like Sidewinder missiles. We finally had to coerce the boards into slowing down before we got to the approaching trees. The wind noise and solid air feeling slowly subsided as we decelerated back to normality and were left thoroughly speed shaken.

We were buzzing from head to toe, and rested a while to take in the 'Nantucket Sleighride' that we had just been on. Lou pointed out some tracks that went in to the woods below us. She said that someone had recently ridden next to a snowboard track through the trees believing that it was a safe route, but failed to see the footprints coming back up. This boarder went straight off the huge cliff hidden by the trees below us, and consequently died in a violent, sad ending.

So we took a known traverse sideways through the woods of epic proportions that seriously burned our calf muscles out. While riding these shaded undulating ruts, I spotted a huge snow hare hopping off into the trees, and wondered how on earth it could survive here? We stopped above a frozen lake and had coffee, and watched some excellent skiers on long, skinny skis doing a tight, steep and deep couloir straight down to the icy lake. I remembered reading that someone had been avalanched there, and unfortunately went through the ice and drowned, and very recently on New Year's Day! God bless them.

After a good rest we rode all the way to the valley bed, and took the crazy bubble car back to the top, as Lou's next plan was to tackle the banana couloir in the Trifides.

On arrival at the couloir entrance it had become a bit icy, possibly due to some guided parties going down it. As we rode into the entrance the descent appeared to be vertical, and the possibility of falling and accelerating into the rocks was high. Its banana shape meant that your fall line would undoubtedly hit rock. Lou was in front, and made a jump turn at the critical part, and nearly lost the edge of her board as it noisily skidded before the metal edge bit into the ice. She carried on, but it had caught me out and I wanted more space between us, so I came to a standstill balanced on one edge of my board, with the thin metal strip just about gripping the ice. My legs shook as I delicately tried to get control of my balance.

Before I knew it a party of skiers that we had just overtaken came down and surrounded me. They were also getting stuck, and the guide was shouting at them, it was instant chaos.

I saw the danger of hitting one of them or vice versa, so I took my back binding out carefully, and edged away from them, and waited. They finally got down far enough away from me to make my move, but putting my binding back on, while the edge of the board gripped the ice, was a different matter. My legs shook again as I tried to pressurise the binding without sending myself plummeting down the slope into severe injury or worse. After a few minutes of the most concentrated subtle work, it clicked in. Relief flooded through me and I made a mental note not to take a binding off like that again, on a very steep slope!

I carefully took off and turned the long board on the ice. I worked my way around the gnarly rocks, overtaking the struggling party, then I flew down the bottom section. I misjudged the angle of the terrain after being on such steep stuff, and shot past Lou, and straight over a load of rocky reefs. I just rode the rocks and kept myself upright, so that the board took the brunt of it. I stopped gingerly and climbed off the rocks. Amazingly the base of the board was only lightly scratched, but that was a gypsy's warning for me.

We rode safely for the rest of the day on different routes down, but as there was so much to explore I decided to come back soon.

At the end of the snow season I returned to La Grave with Lou and tackled more of the challenging terrain. On that day we decided that the Trifides couloirs were too icy to be fun rides, particularly in the light of my last experience and the current conditions, so we fortuitously chose other routes. Another excellent day riding some formidable runs, and some steep and deep white stuff, was only marred in late afternoon when, in the distance, we watched a helicopter landing near the Trifides, which usually indicated a serious issue. At the time we were sat having tardy coffees, looking at the changing sky as a chilly vanilla strip expanded on the horizon before taking our final descent down in the fast freezing snow.

While driving back to Serre Che I reflected on the day, the late helicopters, and how the reputation of La Grave had come about. 'Underestimate it at your peril and pray that the mountain will be your guide, and not your nemesis,' went through my mind, and so did, 'Wild Mountain honey!'

In the bar that night we heard the terrible news that the helicopters had been for a British-based woman, called Lucy Dicker, who had died tragically in the banana couloir of the Trifides. She had recently completed a world trip with her boyfriend. This entailed skiing every day of the year around the world, and a newspaper published a daily report of their journey. After that demanding challenge, she was in La Grave for some end of season skiing, when the accident happened on the icy critical part of that infamous banana couloir. La Meige had claimed another adventurer before the day was out, and injured a few more, but I had a nagging feeling that I knew her name from somewhere else.

When I returned home I spoke to Eddie about her and he was also upset by the news, as we had used her company, Tour Alp, to organise some big BSA trips to the snow and he knew her well. God bless her too. Snowboarding in La Grave seemed somewhat like it would be to surf somewhere heavy, like the North Shore in Hawaii.

The more time I spent searching for good powder, the more of a powder nose I developed. I was getting the ability to sense which areas of the mountain would work, but I also knew that I was riding in avalanche prone territory a lot. I had to rely on my instincts, and boarding partners, to try and avoid getting caught in them. I had a bit of a reputation for avalanching that intrepid photographer Sang Tan, thanks to Eddie and his magazine. Admittedly, I had sent a few avalanches his way on the few occasions we went for an off-piste shoot, but I always made my turn to one side of him with the aim of just missing him, if I set one off!

The locals in Serre Che had a theory that if you went straight at the top, and didn't turn for as long as possible, you could avoid the classic avalanche, usually set off by your weight at the top of a slope under tension. However, like sharks, avalanches are unpredictable, and have to be accepted as part and parcel of these activities. If I got a bad feeling inside, then I would listen to it, and that became an important part of my philosophy. The cost of reaching these amazing highs on the mountain or in the ocean is the risk of injury or death. Sometimes nature wins.

Going back to my office job after that experience was a complete comedown, except that I needed to rest the overworked muscles. I relived these latest escapades by writing articles on Kafi, and another one on La Grave for *SUK*, and made more trips there to respectfully ride the majestic steep slopes. I managed to avoid the avalanches and crevasses, but that was probably more luck than judgement.

Sitting in the office sometimes gave me the opportunity to reason why the activities I did were so fulfilling and exciting. The issue that I often thought about was the definition of perfection? Does it really exist, and why is it so rare? In surfing supposed perfection would be a medium to large wave, with a light offshore breeze to hold the wave up, and dimples on the shiny curved surface, along with a blue sky and no crowds! In snowboarding it would be dry deep fresh powder, with steep terrain and great shapes to turn off, or get air from, and blue sky. These conditions are hard to find, but when you do achieve them they give you an amazing high that lasts for a long time.

There are variations on these conditions that are good, but don't give you the same high. Then there are downright appalling conditions that may give you the buzz of physical activity, but not the extras. An icy piste, or a howling onshore wind, and mushy waves and grey skies, cannot give you that super high of perfection. Although, an added dimension is that you are in the natural world, and your medium is nature, and what if you could take the sea or snow away and see yourself riding through the air? Would it look much different to a great day? Probably not but when you do converge with perfect nature to make this highest of highs, words are useless.

Our man-made attempts to reproduce snow slopes and waves are at early development stages, but for some reason at the moment they don't quite match the feeling that nature gives you. Will they never be able to match nature, as it is fabricated and therefore unnatural? Is something vital missing from the picture like unpredictability, wildlife or dangers?

Size still matters, big waves, big air and big mountains. The search is also a part of it, and change is integral to humans, in this regard. Boredom comes with repetition, and perfection has to be chased, and once found you can try and repeat the long process, or move on with that experience under your belt. Eventually the battle with age truly becomes the next big challenge and nature wins again!

Chod once described snowboarding to a skateboarder, as being like skateboarding in a dream. A soft and fluffy place where you could go anywhere, and jump as high as you liked. You could empower nature, and ride miles down slopes at high speeds. A totally euphoric feeling! That was as good a description as I had ever heard.

My desire to surf the best had diminished due to reaching my limits, overcrowded surf breaks, and the need to chase the wind, tide and swell like a bloodhound. So I just surfed when there was time, and accepted imperfection in the waves, and myself. But I still tried to get the best snow conditions that I could for brief slots in the year, and besides the forays to the Alps or Canada, this was possible locally in the Brecon Beacons. But, I was being dragged deeper into another world, that I was not au fait with, and had never any plans to be in… 'Politics.'

The very word summons images of grey boring people, forever arguing about anything. Never reaching perfection, but always compromising, and so far from the search for perfection in nature, as well. I suppose that they also wanted perfection, but for their egos, bosses, or anyone else with an interest, financial or not, or maybe they just wanted the perfect bank balance.

CHAPTER TWENTY-ONE — 1980 to 1984

— MEN IN GREY SUITS —

"Soft snowflakes call, 'come and play.'
'We'll hug you tight, and let you go, one day!'

In any new sporting activity a plethora of associations and political bodies soon develop in an organic, but sometimes a cockeyed way. Skiing had been around for thousands of years, primarily as a means of crossing snow, and then as a competitive sport over many decades. Therefore, it had enough time to develop slowly, going through many structural and political changes. It had also evolved slowly within the olympic world (I use the small 'o' on purpose), whereas snowboarding was the brand-new, naughty cousin on the block and had its own disparate agenda. It was too premature to exactly define that agenda due to its own dynamic evolution, and this created confusion with the established ski and olympic bodies.

In the beginning the ski bodies thought that snowboarding was a fad, which would quickly disappear. Then, as it flew like an eagle, they had to rethink it, and coincidentally, skiing had peaked in numbers in the '70s, and was declining for many areas. Snowboarding was on an upward curve, and predictions wildly exaggerated dominance on the slopes, at some point in the future. Therefore, a theoretical time would come when there would be a crossing point of the numbers skiing, with those snowboarding. This was a serious threat to the way ski bodies operated, and obtained funds etc. The 'snow sports' financial cake would not easily be shared with these rebellious upstarts, especially as skiing was long established and trapped in the past. And at the end of the day, it's money that drives competitions and sport development, in a complex tangle of commercial and political interests. Then spread it over a lot of countries, with varying interest in snow sports, and it gets even more complicated. Men in grey suits plot and plan how to achieve sporting success, but with their own interests mainly in mind.

So how did all the existing snowboard bodies develop at this early stage? Well, each snowboarding nation quickly started some sort of club or association, just as we had done in the UK. From 1982 onwards there were numerous National Associations primarily in places with snowy mountains. These organising grass roots boarders coordinated the various activities that were required like teaching, general knowledge, trips, and competition.

Then the uniting bodies went through a complicated evolution to link up the world of snowboarding. After the first World Championships in the USA and Europe in 1986/87, the Snowboarders European Association (SEA) was formed, and in

America the North American Snowboarders Association (NASBA) created. These acted for the competitors and went on to organise the official world cups.

Then around 1989, the International Snowboard Association (ISA) was founded to bring together all the nations. But the Americans and Japanese left this venture, so the Professional Snowboarders Association (PSA) was formed for professional racers only.

The PSA and ISA organised the European circuit, and America and Japan had their own circuits – finally the three continents then united to make a world circuit. However, they needed one world governing body, so in 1991 the International Snowboard Federation (ISF) was created. This became the umbrella organisation and ran the World Championships very successfully, for a number of years. The ISA was a partner in the ISF.

It was into this cauldron that I was thrown, as Jeremy no longer wanted to represent the BSA on the ISA/ISF meetings, and Eddie was too busy with the magazine. They asked me if I could go to the next meeting in Germany! Looking back I wonder if I was stitched up!

So I went to meet our European cousins in a mountain hotel in the German Alps, and was pleased to find they were mainly laid back, casually dressed snowboarders. The differences between us and them were that in the UK we had the big dry slope scene, and most Brits were in soft boots, and into freestyle.

The Europeans were much more Alpine orientated and more serious about competition, especially racing. Along with our amateur fun approach to snowboarding, we were definitely lower down their pecking order. We were running the organisation of snowboarding on a shoestring, while the snowy countries were at a higher level, and much closer to each other organisationally and physically. They had to represent more people who wanted to make a career and living from snowboarding, but they still had an underlying philosophy to try and keep the fun aspect. However, the central Europeans seemed to be more rigid than us and formed an inner core to the European scene.

Their use of English was superb, and they used the odd word that I hadn't even heard of. Impressively, they could switch into 'Beavis and Butt-Head' imitations during meetings and lighten things up. However, when a plate of varied local cuisine arrived in front of me, with two fried eggs on top, I had to exclaim, 'that's the dog's bollocks!' There was much frowning and muttering, and then one of them said, 'What's wrong with it?' 'Nothing' I replied. 'It's great!'

This kicked off a big discussion on how the dog's bollocks was a good thing, and not a bad thing, as they had assumed. I seemed to be introducing a new layer to their comprehensive English!

Overall the meeting was positive, and encouraged new ideas for competition to make it more fun and entertaining for competitors, and spectators too. Racetracks with jumps and banks were discussed, and agreed to be introduced. Exciting additions were developing in the snowboard world that would lead to boardercross, slopestyle and more extreme events, alongside the racing and half-pipe. We played with innovative ideas to encompass all the aspects of riding.

The first Junior World Championships were in the planning stage, and new TV rights were opening up the world. Sponsorship was also expanding to new levels, to enable better-organised events for this world stage. We were certainly going on a different path to skiing, and I went back to the UK and wrote up the minutes for Eddie to be published in his magazine. As it was deemed a success, I had just got myself a new unpaid job to add to the list!

Then in 1994, I was lucky enough to go on a trip to Helsinki, in Finland, for another important meeting. I boarded a full plane flying on Finn Air, and on board was a large group of Scottish football supporters, attending an International match in Finland. After all the 'flying on Finn air' jokes wore off, I queried where they would be staying in Helsinki, and they had already decided that it would all depend on the price of Finnish beer. If it was too expensive, then they had been told to catch a ferry to Estonia, for much cheaper beer and to stay there, and then they could get a ferry back for the day of the match.

I took a liking to this bunch of football fanatics, and as I had nothing to do for hours that evening I went with them to the first bar to check the renowned extreme beer prices of Scandinavia. In a large hotel bar the first round was ordered, and the prices declared sane. I had got the third round in as I was going to move on to my hotel, and as I drank up to leave one of the lads had ordered the next round, and to his surprise the price had doubled! We had unwittingly hit happy hour, and it was now over.

They were going to Estonia, which I knew little about, so we parted company. I wandered down the dock area, and was surprised to see a large Russian submarine parked there, and it had been captured in Finnish waters. I was now next to the Russian bear, and could feel the ice-cold wind blowing from its frozen plains.

The next day we started our very important meeting with many nationalities present, and our snowboarding world had been hit by a bombshell. Earlier that year, the skiing world body (FIS), and the olympic committee (IOC), had decided that the FIS would run snowboarding, and that snowboarding would be in the 1998 Olympic Games in Nagano, Japan. No discussion had taken place with the ISF, just a press release to announce their takeover of our sport. It was very hard to take in, and created a lot of instant deep anger. Basically, they wanted to make snowboarding a discipline of skiing, now that it suited them!

This was the very news I had long dreaded and had suspected may happen, as it threw up so many issues and problems, and the focus would now be on this battle, rather than running snowboarding as we had been doing. Despite all these potential problems, we were a united group of different nationalities that all snowboarded. Attending the meetings for the first time was an Estonian snowboard organiser, who gave a talk on his country and how he had taught windsurfing, which allowed some brave souls to escape the USSR, by windsurfing across the Baltic.

'Hell, it was certainly a different world to the one I inhabited,' I thought as he casually explained his experiences.

However, as it was the last week of Russian troop withdrawal from Estonia, under the huge changes taking place in the USSR, he invited the meeting to his excited country. Before I knew it, after the long day meeting, we were on a large ferry leaving Helsinki in the dark, heading for Tallinn in Estonia. We had been allocated cabins, as these ferries drifted in the Baltic in the night to be in duty-free waters, and the whole boat has a party before sailing into Tallinn.

The ship's disco was huge, and had a high open area with long tubes of liquid bubbles that changed colour. You could look down on the dance floor from the mezzanine floor above it, and not wanting to dance, most of us hung out up there watching the fun, and it was certainly different to what I had expected. After a few hours, I staggered to the nearby toilet, and as I was about to walk out the most drunken Viking on the boat walked in. He swayed in front of me, displaying thick bare biceps, and eyes that struggled to focus. He pulled back his big fist, and tried to steady his swaying body. I froze. My mind went blank. I had no action plan, so I left it to my automatic responses. Crazily, I drew a slow finger across my throat, as if I was a part of the mafia! The Viking swayed a bit more, then swivelled slightly, and let the big fist fly past my head into the toilet door. There was a loud splintering noise, and I shot past him before the noise had even stopped.

Heart beating I rejoined the others, but felt on edge now. After a nervous wait for the drunken Viking, who must have probably passed out by then, I told them it was time for bed, and disappeared from the bizarre disco.

In the early grey light, the ship slid over the dark sombre waters of the Baltic, which reflected the hungover passengers on board. A bitter wind blew from Russia, and Tallinn harbour was drab, and very run down too. We boarded a coach, with a large cracked windscreen, that had clearly seen better days. Machine gun toting, armed uniformed police came on, and took all the passports away, except mine. I had been singled out for some reason. The Estonian rep then explained that they had a reciprocal agreement with the UK, so there was no need to check my passport. Well I don't think anyone in the UK knew that, but I bet the Scottish lads were happy about that, as well as the cheap beer.

On the coach journey we saw Russian troops on the move, and we saw the endless grey tower blocks outside of the centre. The rep gave us a lot of information on their situation, and we began to understand how difficult it had been for individualism – especially in alternative sports – to flourish under Kremlin rule. Also, it would still be difficult in the future, as Russia was unpredictable at best, and many Russians had settled in Estonia. He took us on to the main market, and I was saddened by some of the people we saw there. A nice housewife was stood near the market entrance in a thick beige coat and headscarf, holding up a can opener. Hours later we went back past her, and she hadn't moved an inch. The biting wind must have chilled her to the bone; she could have been my mother and I regret not buying a can opener from her to this day.

The old town was very different, and even in the cold grey weather displayed character and charm. We were kindly shown around by our rep, warts and all, and I liked Tallinn and the people that lived there. Then it was back on the disco ferry to Helsinki and more very drunk Scandies, after an enlightening visit to a fast-changing country.

After a difficult lengthy meeting in Helsinki, we all had a lot of work to do on returning to our respective countries, and many more meetings were planned. So, a few days after returning back to work and normality, I was sat in Channel View reflecting on the political problems and writing my notes up ready for more British meetings. I put the evening news on, and there to my horror was the very dock where I had just been sat in a coach with a cracked windscreen! One of those huge disco ferries, 'the Estonia,' had sunk there, and the body count was big. I was stunned and struggled to comprehend it, as that dark vast cold sea had claimed eight hundred and fifty-two lives, it certainly put political sports issues, and the frailty of life, in perspective. I wondered why these aggressive organisations didn't get it, and I felt so sorry for all those people, except maybe the drunken violent Vikings!

CHAPTER TWENTY-TWO — 1994 to 1995

— GAYS ON TRAYS V PRICKS ON STICKS (feat. IOC) —

'Your tracks don't lie!'

The thrill I had snowboarding and surfing was now being cocooned in the intensifying political battle with the skiing and olympic bodies. Some intangible emotion created by these fun activities had slipped away from my life. I was not enjoying riding and surfing as fully as I once did. The political problems had become far more dominant, and just like rust that never sleeps were not going away, and would probably terminate in a 'winner takes all' blunt clash. Now it would be an uphill battle.

I tried to fathom out in simple terms what the hell was going on with these 'sports' bodies? I knew that the average snowboarder wouldn't easily get the complexities of the situation, and probably didn't care too much about it anyway.

It was clearly known that the ISF (International Snowboard Federation) represented the roots snowboarders, and we in the UK were a part of it. They were doing a fairly good job of running snowboarding competition, and they were seamless with the roots of the participants. The difficulties of running a world sporting body were being met, and the majority of competitors were happy. Finances were probably the biggest problem, and controlling the allocation of these limited funds very important. Overall the organisation was heading in the right direction with the philosophy of 'snowboarding for snowboarders.'

The FIS (Federation internacional du Ski) represented the skiers in a much more rigid and rule-bound organisation, and they had the appearance of powerful high-flying business power mongers and seemed far removed from us snowboarders.

The IOC (International Olympic Committee) controlled everything about the olympics, particularly who was allowed to participate in their esteemed games. A quick glance at their chequered history will reveal many allegations of corruption, some proven, some not. The olympic controllers appeared to me to be like an untouchable, autocratic powerful body, tainted by power and money, with little external policing.

So to summarise this new conflict from the information that I gleaned from meetings and newsletters available at the time, it appeared to be as follows:

- Skiing was declining, while snowboarding was expanding and visually far more exciting for younger people, and proclaimed as the fastest growing sport in the world.
- FIS were indifferent to, or hated snowboarding, but saw it as a threat that

could be put under their control. Especially, as the snowboarders ISF had applied for snowboarding to be in the 2002 Olympics, which would have given time for the fledgling sport to develop properly.

- FIS and the IOC were close, and one FIS committee member was on the IOC committee. Therefore, between them they could control how and when a snow sport got into the olympics. FIS had way more money and power than the fledgling ISF.

- Grundig had lost the ISF snowboard world cup sponsorship to Ballantines, and Grundig saw an alternative opportunity to sponsor a FIS snowboard world cup, maybe in retaliation. It was stated by the ISF that Grundig had nudged FIS to start the takeover!

- The IOC needed a youthful image at the olympics to attract younger audiences and advertisers (and therefore more money). Skiing was no longer doing that for them.

- Both the IOC and FIS were initially reluctant, but could see the potential of forcing the ISF out of it and controlling this new sport. Money and power suited both of them, and the ISF was a growing threat to that.

- FIS decided that they could run snowboarding if they put it into the earlier 1998 Olympics, and forced all competitors to go through their own world cup. That was despite snowboarding being underdeveloped in competition format. Consequently the IOC then put snowboarding into the earlier 1998 Nagano games. This also meant that snowboarding would jump the long queue of sports waiting for years to be in the olympics. It would not even be the normal demonstration sport first!

- The IOC would not recognise any competitions organised by the ISF, so riders would have to go through the non-existent FIS races!
- FIS knew that the desire for a gold medal, or olympian status would split the snowboard competition world, and the fast approaching deadline to enter would be the ramifying wedge.

And in a nutshell that was how it panned out over a few years, as the FIS argued that they ran all snow sports, and therefore had to run snowboarding. Although they did not run the snow sliding sport of Biathlon! Also nobody from the snowboarding world had asked them to run snowboarding! This was a premeditated plan, hatched furtively, and probably between connections in the upper echelons of their world. Time was one of their weapons, as competitors would have to decide whether to enter this fast approaching Nagano olympics or not. There was obviously fear in the minds of competitors at missing this 'great' opportunity.

When you strip back the bullshit that came out from these bodies it was obvious what the core reason was for all this palaver. The takeover was to gain money and power from the expanding snowboard world, and at the same time, they could also prevent the loss of power and money from the declining sport of 'skiing.'

So the battle commenced between the ISF and the FIS, and initially lawyers were appointed by the ISF, and Jake Burton, from Burton snowboards, in order to try and stop this unwanted takeover. However, the behaviour of FIS and the olympic committee appeared to be more immoral rather than illegal, and the lawsuit was later dropped.

The FIS started running snowboard competitions very badly, and used a different system to the ISF to pay and sponsor riders. The trade and general riders were not happy with the situation, but the competitors were torn. The FIS system meant that some second tier snowboard competitors had a lot to gain financially from switching from the snowboard world to the FIS, especially compared to the existing top tier riders. Then, when the top riders decided to boycott the olympics, the second tier riders saw a chance like no other.

The best freestyle rider in the world, Terje Haakonsen, said at the time that he would boycott the olympics, because the FIS rules were inappropriate for snowboarding. However, that only led to another pretender to the throne, who would take this opportunity to be famous. In fact, it helped many competitors if the best were not there competing, despite it being a hollow gold for them. You can milk a gold, whichever way it is gained!

There were attempts by the ISF to compromise, and some events became jointly recognised, like the ISF Continental Open in Thredbo, Australia. The political situation in each country was, however, very different, which led to much confusion. It soon became apparent that agreements were being broken in some countries, and the divisive plan becoming exposed. Clearly, the snowboarder's representatives, the ISF, could no longer trust, or run parallel with the skiing body. The ISF newsletter reported that 'they had felt the cold breath of the Beast for the first time – called dirty politics.'

If this had the appearance of a big business taking out a small one, then that's because, basically, it was that, but with sporting bodies, supported by big bucks sponsors! What went on from that point was a nasty split between those that wanted to go to the olympics, and those that said their principles wouldn't allow them to go and compete. Viewpoints were chosen through the prism of information from sports bodies, and what came through the grapevine, as the general media had little interest in this situation. The actions of the FIS/IOC threw a long shadow over snowboarding from this point onwards and it felt like there was poison in the well.

We wasted a lot of energy, time, and money, battling the FIS and IOC, but we honestly thought that there was a chance of people pulling together, but it was clear that the shifty, elusive entrance to the underworld was open for business. Some resorts were forced to take FIS snowboard events, or else they would lose any existing FIS skiing events, and also they weren't allowed to put on any ISF events. Pressure was also put on National skiing bodies to run snowboarding, but each one was in a different situation, causing much confusion.

Eddie wrote in *SUK*: 'Ludicrous. You'll be pleased to know that most ski bodies have treated this with the contempt it deserves, practically ignoring it, preferring to allow their country's snowboard associations to get on with it. This is the situation with the British Ski Federation and the British Snowboard Association in Britain. FIS have blown it.'

It was here that Eddie and I differed, as I saw human nature from another viewpoint. When some of the country's skiing bodies disagreed with the FIS I thought that just maybe there was a slim chance. However, the childhood olympic daydream of being hailed a hero on the podium, would be too much for some. The big stick of the olympics and funding could also be used by FIS against their own national bodies. In my view it would just be a matter of time and uncertainty; before their masters imposed their will on them. God only knows what other discreet ploys were used by the FIS and IOC during this time?

The lure of gold and desire of becoming an olympian would certainly be too powerful for some. FIS too were powerful and had the money and resources to throw at the sport, whereas the ISF were not subsidised, and it was more expensive to compete on their world cup. Money talks, big egos need satisfying and we all have secret, atavistic daydreams that steer us along life's path. Goldie looking medals!

— OLYMPIC DREAM RANT —

"He alone, who owns the youth,
gains the future.' – Hitler

Sometimes I would wake in the morning and forget that this crazy political saga was happening, then something would trigger in my mind about the reality of some distant bunch of 'sports suits' affecting our future. As this future that we were now in was nothing like the collective vision we had dreamt of, or expected, my own view as a non-competitor was uncompromising. If I had of been competing and offered the chance to go to the olympics I would have said 'No!' Nein, Non, Ez, Na, Ne, Nee, Nei, Nei, Nej, Ei, Lie, 'A'ole, Nao, or whatever.

I had been a part of the work and energy put into the growth of snowboarding and watched it amazingly expand across the UK, and to far flung places. I had lived in a region where snowboarding didn't even exist when I made my first boards, a bit like giving birth to it, and a painful one too! I think that if I were cut open, the word 'snowboard' would run through one side of me like a stick of rock, and the other side would have 'surf' going through it. Just like some surfers and skaters that I know, though some people have the word 'money,' or 'fame' going through them.

When one of the American ISF organisers, Ted Martin, defected from the ISF to the FIS, it was apparent that the snowboard world would be permanently split. Ted Martin was once a skier that competed, but did not have the skill to have made the olympics, as was his dream. After becoming an organiser of sporting events he was somehow involved in the formation of the snowboard body, the ISF. Even at that early stage Eddie had met him at an ISF meeting, and felt that he didn't fit in with the existing snowboard mindset. Now, by switching sides at a crucial moment, he could go to the olympics through the back door, as he took an offer he thought that he couldn't refuse, to the detriment of others.

His defection, and others, allowed the FIS to get properly organised and, although the IOC had once 'indicated' that both ISF and FIS riders should be able to enter, FIS could now close the door on the ISF, as they no longer needed any of their expertise to run snowboard competitions.

The impact of all this upon my life was to be sent to various meetings across Europe and report back on our revised plan of action. One such meeting was organised in Innsbruck, Austria in April of 1996. The ISF had launched a joined up initiative to strengthen the snowboard world under the banner 'Planet Snowboard'. This was a big meeting attended by a lot more boarders than usual and a big party in town had been organised. By that I mean a party that involved a couple of hundred people with music and international chatter. On top of that attraction my snowboard buddy from Gloucester, Carl Ringelberg, was going to meet me there.

Innsbruck was blessed with warm sunshine on arrival. I quickly showered and put my best casual clothing on and excitedly went out to meet Carl. We sat in the late hazy sun outside of a pristine café and chin-wagged for a couple of hours and lined our stomachs for the forthcoming escapade. Carl had overdone it a bit with the Jean Paul Gaultier, and the sweet smell still lingers in my mind years later! The first drinks sunk without a trace, and soon the night was in full swing. Snowboard contacts of all sorts were reuniting or meeting for the first time and a high-energy buzz filled the place. Slowly the party descended into drunken groups of loose friends bouncing around and making unintelligible attempts at each other's languages. It was a late, fun night by any standards.

The next day, breakfast was a sombre affair attended by the few that made it, and those that did were only to be greeted by plates of salami and other unsuitable meats for this time in the morning. I met up with Carl, who had clearly consumed far too much schnapps at the end of the night, as he was a whiter shade of pale whilst he slowly sipped his black coffee. We found the venue for the meeting which was a large conference hall with a view over the recently snow bound, pale grass outside. More coffee was our first priority and then we found some seats ready for the start of the meeting.

The usual introductions and update on where world snowboarding was at currently were completed and the idea behind Planet Snowboard explained. Both myself and the speaker couldn't help noticing that Carl had changed colour several times from white to green and all shades in between. When Carl went a purply shade of green and got up to go and be sick, the speaker had to say how impressed he was with the psychedelic facial show that he had been watching! Once the long morning was over and only I had the stomach to tackle lunch, we sat outside in the sun. The energy sapping night out was catching up on us fast and on returning to the meeting I felt sleepy, weary and still a bit hung over.

The meeting started with some droll stuff about the behaviour of the olympic committee and our actions to date, but we already knew all of this. The speaker droned on and on until my eyelids went as heavy as hell, suddenly there was a commotion outside on the grassy area, although nobody got up or took much notice, in fact the speaker professionally ploughed on, so I quietly slid out of my seat and walked out and around the building to the sizeable grassy expanse at the side. To my horror there were nine, shiny, stark-naked warriors covered in grease larking about and chatting and pushing each other around.

They were assembling for a running race to a large olive tree about two hundred metres away. A distracted crowd of men and boys noisily conversed between mouthfuls of meat and wine. I stared at the cheekiest runner with thick dark hair and couldn't help noticing a strong resemblance to Cammy Bain, the Scottish snowboarder. Then I noticed the tall, more aloof athlete, with long black hair and a moustache who looked remarkably like Huw Parsons from Outdoor Action!

The race finally started to cheering and jeering bystanders, as their floppy parts bounced around in the dash for the sacred olive tree of Zeus. *Blimey*, I thought. *This must be the first olympics*. It bore an amazing similarity to the first British snowboard championships!'

The winner was adorned with an olive wreath and unsurprisingly it was the lean one that looked like Huw Parsons who had won, and he could now keep walking tall with quiet confidence. The Cammy Bain looking one came last and had to keep up the joking and fooling about! Then these justified and ancient athletes all went to duly pay their respects to Zeus the sender of thunder, lightning, rain and winds in the nearby temple.

In a flash, the years slid by and the religious festival became more games-orientated but the competitors were still naked. The first arena was built to seat interested watchers, and I viewed, in disbelief, as chariots raced around a rough track in chaos, causing injuries and death to great applause from the hostile crowd. Slippery naked warriors wrestled and boxed to the point of no return and sometimes an entrant had to be carried away for a premature funeral.

Then a huge figure of a Roman emperor appeared in the middle of the chaos and announced that this four yearly religious and games event was to be abolished as it was too pagan for these modern times. Its run of over a thousand years was done and dusted, these Gods were now unwanted and unneeded.

One thousand five hundred years flew by without the religious games, until someone in England started an idea to revive these games, and a Frenchman followed it up, which led to a bunch of Edwardian looking fellows restarting the Olympics in Athens. Starchy men in long white shorts, white shirts, all sporting moustaches like Huw Parsons, had lined up to run the straight track. They were off and their new credo was 'The most important thing in the olympic games is not to win but to participate.' Cool, I think?

Then, as thousands gathered in the Berlin stadium, Adolf Hitler, called the youth of the world, well only certain youth! I watched as Jesse Owens ran and jumped to four golden medals and Hitler looked like he had bitten a lemon! The political conniving going on behind the scenes would have been entirely at home in the Roman senate. There was a nasty smell in the air, and the political organisers were out of tune with the rhythms of the balanced world.

And so it sped on until men in grey suits arrived and various nationalities passed brown envelopes stuffed with money around, like pass the parcel, until a new venue was chosen around the globe. This created jobs, unwanted buildings, debt, environmental issues and greed. The athletes were now less important than the suits and a huge television above the stadium signified where money was coming and going. Athletes now trained full-time and got paid by someone, the credo had changed and winning was everything! Losers were of no interest to the media, unless they were strangely flawed or did something sensationally newsworthy.

A loud clatter of falling coffee cups brought me back into the General Assembly of snowboarders. It was coffee time again and by Zeus I needed it as I had just witnessed something incredible in a field in Innsbruck, a potted journey through the olympics. I wouldn't have called it an olympic dream though, more of an olympic daydream, my olympic daydream, warts and all.

The new ideas for snowboarding being proposed by the speakers were good, but had probably come too late to keep snowboarding being run by snowboarders, and anyway, all of these good ideas would probably be stolen! I took the necessary notes to report back to the BSA committee in the UK and we gratefully left for the day.

Chatting in the bar afterwards, while Carl sipped fruit juices and tried to explain the inner workings of his Land Rover Defender, I half-listened to a rap song on the sound system until slowly the words altered in my mind freshly filled with politics, and my thoughts synced with the music.

Y' old farts thought you had it made!
Until you saw your income fade!
Olympic spirit went down the pan,
Quick as a flash or a sprinting man.

More public, more money's the game
Control the youth with plastic fame,
Divide and rule 'n create a fight
Slyly, slowly just like a great white.

You lov'd them ancient naked Greeks,
But 'Democrazy' don't fit you geeks,
Grabbing free lunch, what a feast
You're the cold breath of da beast.

Sanitise our lifestyle, won't you
And turn it upside down, don't you
What's a goldie-looking medal worth?
Compared to your finan'shall girth?

Synchronised tiddley winks that's next?
Genetically tested for drugs and sex,
Moola, cash, loot, bread and honey,
Higher, faster, stronger, money.

You didn't want to know the roots?
You only want the winners fruits?
Better cheat than lose, won't you
Selling olympic spirit, aren't you!

The song suddenly ended and my mind was

dragged back into a Land Rover engine, as Carl was still on a roll with his intimate machine love. Finally Carl and I parted company after a mega weekend, and I took my new information back to the UK, mainly for the few of us that this would really affect, the organisers and competitors.

On the flight back I had time to reflect on this crazy weekend. All I knew was that surfing and snowboarding had brought about my closeness to the planet. I owed them this debt and wouldn't go down without a fight, despite the inevitability of being swallowed and regurgitated by the skiing and olympic bodies in their pain trap. Although we were in a fight for our existence as snowboard organisers, our own competitors were switching sides will-nilly. This made me wonder why on earth I was fighting for them and their egos and the next wave of defectors. For my part I was losing my desire to spend my spare time and stress myself out with all this dry political stuff. I was in place where I was not happy, and that goddam dog had stitched me up, good and proper.

I hazarded a guess that the pioneers of snowboarding would probably slowly disappear into domesticity or go into dull jobs selling things. The old farts would stay at the helm pocketing the profits and free lunches, laying down endless rules for the competitors. Snowboard fashion would be diluted and skiing would pinch the snowboard spirit and the farts would try to become more hip. It was all so predictable, but strange times indeed.

Although I did like to wonder where it all would have gone if we had remained together, united like in a John Lennon song. That would have been a tough one for the ski bodies and olympic suits to have cracked, but money and power always wins over in the end. I was not from the skiing world, like many, and would never have skied. Even though in the early days of my surfing experience 'old man Gwyn,' who surfed and skied, would sit on his board out the back at sunny Llangennith and tell me tales in between the sets of rounded waves coming in. He loved gesticulating and enthusiastically explaining how you could ski miles down a mountain to a little village below you in the Austrian Alps. Then he would encourage me to learn to ski on one of Rogers's big trips, but it was not my cup of tea, as they say. And funnily enough, Gwyn switched to snowboarding when I started teaching at the Swansea slope, so he was a true surfer at heart.

As expected, over the next four years, the slow demise of snowboarding's original organisers happened and the skiing body controlled who went to snowboard in the olympics. I now wondered where my olympic t-shirt was from all those years ago when I really needed it? So, perhaps now 'Snowboarding was for sheep.'

CHAPTER TWENTY-FOUR — 1999 ONWARDS

— SLIP SLIDING AWAY —

'Snow Karma – Kings that lost their crowns!'

I owed snowboarding a debt and I felt that it owed me one. We were tied like lovers, able to part, but a parcel of our souls would not separate. I knew that the 'snowboarding run by snowboarders' philosophy had generally failed. The impact of the FIS/IOC decision had been to alter that fun matrix of characters that had evolved snowboarding from its roots permanently, exchanging the laid-back ambience of competition for a rule bound environment. I sensed that the authenticity of the snowboard culture would now feel fabricated, and full of even more media clichés. I didn't feel angry, as much as disillusioned by the stitched up world that we lived in. We would be a discipline of skiing, second-class and run by unknowns or defectors, probably sat around in central European five-star hotels, rubbing their wallets. Consequently, sports presenters on TV, in suits and ties, would talk about snowboard tricks, in a plastic way, and ski and snowboard presenters would fawn over each other's sports, and so on.

I realised that talking endlessly about a sport, and not doing it was now not for me, the Dodo had fortunately become extinct before it became a McDodo. Although we had lost this battle, I guess so had all those that switched sides and did not get their fantasy win. Only the ones with gold or silver were really 'winners' as far as the media were concerned, and even that was contentious. The organisers and sponsors could now create the image that they wanted, and I didn't want to be a provocateur on the inside, nor could I prostitute myself. The control from the top down would now be able to influence the grass roots, not the other way round, as in the early days. Power and money was the real winner, the new olympic spirit, veiled behind closed doors for the foreseeable future. I was however very disappointed in the people, and organisations, that tolerated just being pawns in this power game. In this great future you can't forget the shrouded past. Back at ya!

Acceptance of the takeover had been happening slowly, so it was not now some sort of shock. However, along the years that I had been participating in this activity, I had watched the slow disintegration of a European country on the TV news.

Yugoslavia was turning in on itself in an incredibly hostile and violent way, and the winter olympic rings were in disarray in Sarajevo. The ski jump commentators box was a UN control room based in the middle of the carnage, and Torvill and Dean's victory site was a scene of heavy shelling and mass graves. Sick of watching it on TV and in a new vacuum, I finally wanted to help in some way, as I was always conscious of the selfish side to the activities that I had 'chosen' to do, which created an endless cycle of energy. By this I mean paddling out against the energy of the waves to ride that energy back in, and going uphill against gravity to snowboard back down using the same gravity. This would probably make sense to a Buddhist monk but it didn't to my bank manager.

So I now had too much time to reflect on the bigger picture of what was happening in the shrinking world of the ascending Internet. I somehow became a temporary aid worker with a motivated, crazy little bunch in a NGO charity. That draw, to a painful place, was a way of experiencing more painful suffering than a divorce, and a breaking away from the snowboard world, which had wasted a lot of energy. Trying to alleviate some suffering was mutually beneficial, to the refugees and myself. There is a saying amongst aid workers that they need the disaster and suffering as much as the refugees, and I could understand it.

Strangely, however, I was able to experience that elusive release of my spirit, like a Douglas Coupland character, in extreme circumstances. It happened during the difficult time spent close to the Kosovo war zone, where gunfire and bombing were daily occurrences, usually at a fairly safe distance.

One dark night a gun went off very near me, probably aimed at me. The sudden bang made my spirit jump clean out of my body, but it was pulled back so quickly, as if it was on an elastic band. It left me with a tingling spine and frozen with fear, but conversely, it had some of the same hallmarks as the best rides I had done both in snowboarding and surfing. My spirit would have gone somewhere else, but my existential body was having none of it!

Once through the darkness of other people's suffering, and my own, I could slowly learn to enjoy surfing and snowboarding again. And enjoy it for the pure fun and high that it gave me, it was like a new dawn and a homecoming. Chod had once told me that he preferred freeriding the mountain to anything else. Despite winning the overall title at the pivotal British Open Championships in Andorra, he said that competing was a different feeling to a great day in fresh powder. He didn't think that you should be judged, and competition shouldn't be as important as freeriding.

So maybe that floating feeling was not at all about winning competitions, which could just be primitive competitive drive, and the pleasure of beating other people, just like our distant ancestors would have behaved to hopefully survive. That floating feeling could be for anybody who breaks free from the mundane routine of life on Earth, who breaks free from gravity for a brief foray into another space, or allows nature to give you a free ride in the now. At this point I was able to balance my two mistresses, without bias, getting the most out of each discipline with a casual ease.

Finding a reliable partner to ride with can be difficult in both sports, so I would often go walkabout up Brecon Beacons on my own, and assess the risk of doing a couloir or steep face, with no worry about anyone else. I enjoyed doing both sports alone for a while, but all that changed when Aussie Pete Williams had unexpectedly knocked the door of Channel View, and I found a reliable partner for both floating worlds. Old friend 'Jonesey' worked alongside Pete in Oz and he had told Pete that he could stay at our place, for free, on his European tour! And a Godsend he was too as he waited in the guesthouse in return for lodgings, and I could cheekily introduce him as my Australian butler!

We surfed together, and he learned to snowboard fast, and after a few trips to the Alps I think that he knew the Snowy Mountains back home wouldn't do it for him. After boomeranging between the UK and Oz, he finally got married and settled in Swansea, and over the years we made plenty of off-piste trips, and managed to surf places like the Canaries, Sri Lanka and locally a lot. We learned to rely on each other, and chase the same aspirations, which led to some great experiences at seriously challenging spots with him, creating new memories on top of those special early ones.

Once I had reached my riding plateau, I was happy to enjoy it and accept my limitations; dash the ego and let go, once the ego is freed from the desire to be 'up there,' it's easier to look around and enjoy yourself. I often remind myself that we are all spinning around on a planet through space and time, travelling at 67,000 miles per hour, and there's absolutely no (corrupt) committee in charge, luckily, but because we cannot feel this incredible force, we think that it's not happening! The sun and stars are not really whizzing across our sky every day, it's just yet another illusion!

However, the bad news is that we only get a short ticket to ride the planet, as it's temporary, and we all have to face our own death! And before that I always wanted to feel that I had been true to myself, and to the spirits of snowboarding and surfing. Those spirits that I first met all those years ago by accident. Soul, hippies, war, punk, skaters, hip hop, skiers, ravers, control freaks, men in grey suits, whatever, had all tried to influence them, but you can find that spirit in the simplicity of riding alone, or with a friend. Stripped of bullshit, and back to the bones, standing sideways, as always, zooming across water, frozen or not, and, preferably, in a natural environment, the very planet that we have inherited. Why destroy what we have for something fabricated? We can only offend Mother Nature for so long before the backlash comes.

That elusive thread of soul and spirit, which had run through snowboarding, had now left the building. Where's it gone now? I don't know, probably where no one is looking, especially the media, but I do know it is not in the FIS or IOC, it was more likely to have followed Terje Haakonsen, the principled world champion who went on to set up the Ticket to Ride (TTR) World Snowboard Tour, in

2002.

British snowboard pioneer Huw Parsons once told me how amazing it was to have ridden the North face of Pen y fan, in South Wales, from top to bottom on a blue-sky day, in powder. It was amazing because it was local and unexpected and therefore carried more kudos, however, I had never seen it in those conditions, despite waiting for many years. Then, one winter's day we had even, deep snow across the Beacons, so Pete and I drove up and parked by the easiest walk up to the highest point.

We had an azure sky, and there was deep powder everywhere across the Beacons, unusually from top to bottom. This was it. I could fulfil another promise to myself, but first we rested to admire the magnificent views northwards over Mid-Wales. We walked over the icy fossilised ripple marks that reminded me that even on this high summit we were still on a beach! With apprehension and excitement, we clambered down some icy rocks facing north and dropped the rest of the way onto the deep snow. Then we flew down the steep snowy face, with the underlying strata causing bumpy waves, and we had to ride on pure instinct and react quickly to changes in the terrain. We were forced to traverse sharply to avoid getting drawn in to the frozen lake, and as I rode I knew that the Swell Panik was in its natural environment, and so was I, and the ride went on forever.

We passed serious hikers midway up, and near the bottom keen young sledders, who had walked up to whiz speedily down. We flew past them all like blurs, until the land levelled off into farms, and we stopped breathlessly, filled with adrenaline, and looked back with great satisfaction at the huge descent we had just accomplished. We were now many miles from the car, and had no intention of walking all the way back up. We didn't care though as we had freed ourselves from the mundane world temporarily. The ride had been an adventure, changing and changing through the varying terrain and snow states. For what we had just done, there were no committees or rules.It had been pure fun in a passing, magical environment.

I thought of Huw and his words, and in many ways, I had always followed him, inadvertently on his path, and trying to reach his dizzy heights, but more so now that I was out of the politics! His words became my words, 'I have seen the future of snowboarding and it's not for me.'

So I just go snowboarding and surfing now, but sometimes I don't know if I am snowboarding or surfing! It's just the emotional state that I reach that matters, and living in the moment, not the future or the past, nor in the bureaucratic layers that pervade this world. Maybe all those very competitions that were organised, and brought us together were the soul-slayers of snowboarding? An inevitable sad syndrome de glissment, so perhaps I was the fool, and should have selfishly just gone riding instead. I had gone from nothing to anything and back, like beautiful losers do!

— EPIDOGUE —

'Your tracks will fade into nothing.'

In winter's dark dip, the deep blues and blacks abound, short days and icy mountains cast long, dark shadows. Beleaguered by the cold, still, unfathomable seas that give birth to the clean bones of the dense waves, the cold sinks deep down into your body, and your bladder. Pete and I catch the odd, good surf session dressed in full dark wet suits, looking like seals, but we also sometimes get to ride the icy slopes of the Alps, or Brecon, in cold blue skies washed with winter colours. Axis tipped away from the sun, even weary birds freeze on their branches, hopeful that spring will break this wilful nadir.

Then, through the cracks, the spring light and green growth explodes, the storms rush in from the Atlantic giving energy to our shores and mountains. The best waves and snow create a feeding frenzy for Pete and I. It's then that I plan our dash to the mountains, while Pete accurately forecasts the best snow week in the Alps. We take bigger risks, and get bigger rewards. It's my favourite time, fresh powder, blue waves, buds and birdsong with a shiny future. Energy creates energy for eternal voyagers.

Summer's dreamy bright colours metamorphose

the scenery to a new flaming high. The chilly sea rapidly warms, and the snow becomes invisible water vapour. The heat melts the boundaries of my mind, and we surf the golden beaches, turquoise seas and obscure reef breaks. The waves fall about foolishly, and the ocean jokes with us and is not intent on harming surfers. Our hearts sing, and only cold beer can help, whilst the boys strum the Azure Summertime Blues, on sunny Langland wall.

In early autumn we surf comforting warm seas and testing big waves. Pete and I have to challenge our fail-sure design as we age against the potent infinite storms. Powerful waves, born in a maelstrom, are created and hell-bent on destruction, they batter the coast. We paddle a lot, eat a lot and tune in to the discordant oceanic rhythms of this distant God. The seasons straddle one another, alternating like the volatile wind, something and nothing. We feel the coming changes in the air, and the visibly shortening days warn of more ebb than flow.

In the late autumn we are slowly stripped down to our soul, and goose pimples appear out of the chilly air. Coloured leaves swirl and twirl, until they optimistically hit the freezing ground in a jigsaw mosaic. We surf with more wetsuit on and ride locally; it all starts closing in on us. Grey days, bare hedges, and early sunsets, create a yearning to pessimistically curl up in front of the TV. The Beacons become ochre shadows of themselves, and project a melancholy like no other season.

And so life goes on; season after season, spiralling through time and space to that unknown secret destination. What was really important when I look back? The planet spins, dogs bite, lilo's pop, and the pinball fires again, and again, and again. A random mystery, an alien laboratory or a pre-ordained plan, it still eludes me? Was all this craziness exactly what that wild dog Blackie had in mind for me when he bite the lilo as a form of karmic punishment, just for not giving him enough freedom and Scooby snacks!? With only my demise certain and the hope of another floating world, obscured from view, I wonder, in between surfing and snowboarding, about the existence of that hidden dimension. Can there be a slippery door leading restless spirits to that floating world briefly encountered, tantalisingly temporary, and experienced within you? Can my swaying belief go beyond hope of another world devoid of human greed, a creative power or complete darkness?

Surely that mysterious place that I came from is where I will end up, and anyway whose master plan are you in?